A VIEW FROM THE BRIDGE

ARTHUR MILLER (1915–2005) was born in New York City and studied at the University of Michigan. His plays include *All My Sons* (1947), *Death of a Salesman* (1949), *The Crucible* (1953), *A View from the Bridge* (1955), *A Memory of Two Mondays* (1955), *After the Fall* (1964), *Incident at Vichy* (1964), *The Price* (1968), *The Creation of the World and Other Business* (1972), and *The American Clock* (1980). He also wrote two novels, *Focus* (1945) and *The Misfits* (1957), which was filmed in 1960, and the text for three books of photographs by Inge Morath: *In Russia* (1969), *In the Country* (1977), and *Chinese Encounters* (1979). He twice won the New York Drama Critics Circle Award, and in 1949 he was awarded the Pulitzer Prize. He was the recipient of the National Book Foundation Medal for Distinguished Contribution to American Letters in 2001, the prize Prince of Asturias of Letters in 2002, and the Jerusalem Prize in 2003.

PHILIP SEYMOUR HOFFMAN is an actor on stage and in film. His movie credits include *Capote*, *Charlie Wilson's War*, and *Doubt*, among others. Stage credits include revivals of Sam Shepard's *True West* and Eugene O'Neill's *Long Day's Journey into Night*. He has been a member of the Labyrinth Theatre Company since 1995. In addition to directing a number of theater productions, he recently made his feature directorial debut with *Jack Goes Boating*.

ARTHUR MILLER

A View from the Bridge

A PLAY IN TWO ACTS

Foreword by
PHILIP SEYMOUR HOFFMAN

Introduction by
ARTHUR MILLER

PENGUIN BOOKS

PENGUIN CLASSICS

Published by the Penguin Group
Penguin Books Ltd, 80 Strand, London WC2R ORL, England
Penguin Group (USA) Inc., 375 Hudson Street, New York, New York 10014, USA
Penguin Group (Canada), 90 Eglinton Avenue East, Suite 700, Toronto, Ontario, Canada M4P 2Y3
(a division of Pearson Penguin Canada Inc.)
Penguin Ireland, 25 St Stephen's Green, Dublin 2, Ireland (a division of Penguin Books Ltd)
Penguin Group (Australia), 250 Camberwell Road, Camberwell, Victoria 3124, Australia
(a division of Pearson Australia Group Pty Ltd)
Penguin Books India Pvt Ltd, 11 Community Centre, Panchsheel Park, New Delhi – 110 017, India
Penguin Group (NZ), 67 Apollo Drive, Rosedale, North Shore 0632, New Zealand
(a division of Pearson New Zealand Ltd)
Penguin Books (South Africa) (Pty) Ltd, 24 Sturdee Avenue, Rosebank, Johannesburg 2196, South Africa

Penguin Books Ltd, Registered Offices: 80 Strand, London WC2R ORL, England

www.penguin.com

First published in the United States of America by The Viking Press 1955
Published in a Viking Compass edition (with a new introduction by the author) 1960
Published in Penguin Books 1977
This edition with a foreword by Philip Seymour Hoffman published by Penguin Group (USA) in 2009
This edition first published in Great Britain by Penguin Classics 2010

014

Copyright © Arthur Miller, 1955, 1957, 1960
Copyright renewed Arthur Miller, 1983, 1985, 1988
Foreword copyright © Philip Seymour Hoffman, 2009
All rights reserved

The moral right of the author of the Foreword has been asserted

CAUTION: Professionals and amateurs are hereby warned that performance of *A View from the Bridge* is
subject to a royalty. It is fully protected under the copyright laws of the United States of America, Canada,
United Kingdom and the rest of the British Commonwealth, and of all countries covered by the Berne
Convention for the Protection of Literary and Artist Works, the Pan-American Copyright Conventions, the
Universal Copyright Convention, and of all countries with which the United States has reciprocal copyright
relations. All rights, including but not limited to professional and amateur stage rights, motion picture,
recitation, lecturing, public reading, television and radio broadcasting, video and sound recording, and the
rights of translation into foreign languages are strictly reserved. Particular emphasis is placed upon the matter
of readings, permission for which must be secured in writing. Inquiries should be addressed to International
Creative Management, Inc., 825 Eighth Avenue, New York, New York 10019.

Lyrics from "Paper Doll" by Johnny Black. Copyright by Edward B. Marks Music Corporation.
Used by permission

Printed in England by Clays Ltd, St Ives plc

Except in the United States of America, this book is sold subject
to the condition that it shall not, by way of trade or otherwise, be lent,
re-sold, hired out, or otherwise circulated without the publisher's
prior consent in any form of binding or cover other than that in
which it is published and without a similar condition including this
condition being imposed on the subsequent purchaser

978-0-141-18996-3

www.greenpenguin.co.uk

FSC
MIX
Paper from
responsible sources
www.fsc.org   FSC™ C018179

Penguin Books is committed to a sustainable
future for our business, our readers and our planet.
This book is made from Forest Stewardship
Council™ certified paper.

Contents

A VIEW FROM THE BRIDGE

Foreword

Sometimes when I'm with friends, or when I'm at work, I'll ask if anyone knows the first line of *Death of a Salesman*. And to be fair, I'll remind them that it's mentioned as a "perhaps" in the stage directions, and does not appear in the dialogue itself. Almost no one ever knows it, which is good for me, because then I get to say it. And when I do I always hope that someone will be taken by it, that I'll inspire someone to understand why it's the saddest of sad moments. Willy Loman arrives home after another halfhearted attempt at trying to drive himself off the road. He sets his bags down and sits at the kitchen table, maybe he has a glass of milk, and he says, "Oh boy." It's only a matter of time. He's too old, possibly going senile, and proud. Willy believes he's worth more dead than alive, and that belief keeps sending him off the road, dreaming of a better life for his wife and two sons. He's been found out, not just for being past his prime but for never having had one. At least not the kind he vividly conjures—playing catch with the boys in the backyard, talking about how "well-liked" (as he is fond of saying) he is in every town and profiting nicely because of it.

I was twelve when I first saw *All My Sons* and fifteen when I lay on the living room couch in the house where I was raised and read *Death of a Salesman*, maturing as I held my breath the way people do when they don't want to miss anything. Of course, getting older and having children and being responsible for more than just myself has only deepened my empathy for Willy, Eddie Carbone in *A View from the Bridge*, Joe Keller in *All My Sons*, and the rest of Miller's characters. Still, I understand as I did back then that none of us really wants to be known, to be exposed, to be found out. We want to keep part of ourselves—the source of our deepest vulnerabilities—hidden, both to ourselves and to others. And yet sometimes, despite our best efforts, our hearts peek out, and we want to sneak off and sit with our heads in our hands and softly let the words "oh boy" exhale out of our mouths. Alfieri, the lawyer in *A View from the Bridge*, puts it perfectly in his tribute to Eddie: "For he allowed himself to be wholly known and for that I think I will love him . . ." We secretly grieve for all who are "wholly known," like Eddie and Willy and Joe. Miller knew that. He knew we would empathize as long as his characters allowed us to see how black things had gotten.

Miller has been said to be confronting the American Dream and its unattainable ideals. I'm sure he was, and I imagine it was quite personal. More specifically, though, he is bringing us uncomfortably close to the tragedy that arises not from our failures alone, but also—and especially—from our failures being laid bare, and laid bare by our own actions. Eddie Carbone sits in the corner of a room facing the wall as we all laugh, grateful we aren't him, relieved our secret is still intact. Eddie wants something that nature won't allow—and I don't mean the all-consuming, unmentionable love for his niece. He wants time to stop. But as long as the days pass and everyone plays their part—as long as *A View from the Bridge* cycles inexorably through its scenes—Eddie will be made known, and we will deny we liked him or even knew him. Time will not stop for him. I remember hearing the phrase "pulled inside out" to describe a man whose masculine exterior has been removed and all that remains is soft and sad and wailing. Eddie is that man, unprotected, revealed, us.

Miller is also writing about that part of us that cannot help itself, that brings us down every day, and eventually for good; that part of us that can't be sated, no matter what we do. He knows how helpless we are against the need to be adored—and I don't mean just accepted or liked but "well-liked," to the point of unattainable fantasy. He knows how weak we are when it comes to love, lust, and pride—a dangerous combination. A friend of mine mentioned how during the 1940s and '50s, when these plays were first produced, the fear of being exposed or found out was greater because the consequences were greater. I thought, sure, but even though Miller was commenting on post-war America and the working class and everything that concerned the laboring, fighting man, what always touched me more than the particulars of their struggles was that they cut to the bone. Their sins may have been prompted or exacerbated by the postwar era or outside circumstances, but in the end the particulars fall away. The tragedy of being "known" in this way is timeless, universal, and unforgiving.

Eddie Carbone's sin is an unspeakable desire, a yearning cloaked in virtue. Willy Loman's is adultery and make-believe, and Joe Keller's is murder, but they fight on as if they can't be seen, like the child who thinks he's invisible just because he covers his eyes. And the more they punch at the air, hoping that time will stop or that it all never happened or that men aren't men and women aren't women and dogs will fly and they will die, the more it's so so hard to watch and so so beautiful and human that you want to scream, "You can't eat the orange and throw the peel away—a man is not a piece of fruit," and grab your hat the way Dustin Hoffman did when he played Willy on Broadway, howling his grief to the back row; or the way Anthony Lapaglia as Eddie flooded the streets with his empty righteous rage, hoping that Catherine would see the story in his head and come back and hold him and stop all this.

Here we find the true compassion and catharsis that are as essential to our society as water and fire and babies and air. I remember walking and running and jumping out of the theater after seeing *Death of a Salesman*, like a child in the morning, because Miller awakened in me the taste for all that must be— the empathy and love for the least of us, out of which bursts a gratitude for the poetry of these characters and the greatness of their creator.

PHILIP SEYMOUR HOFFMAN

Introduction

A play is rarely given a second chance. Unlike a novel, which may be received initially with less than enthusiasm, and then as time goes by hailed by a large public, a play usually makes its mark right off or it vanishes into oblivion. Two of mine, *The Crucible* and *A View from the Bridge*, failed to find large audiences with their original Broadway productions. Both were regarded as rather cold plays at first. However, after a couple of years *The Crucible* was produced again off Broadway and ran two years, without a line being changed from the original. With McCarthy dead it was once again possible to feel warmly toward the play, whereas during his time of power it was suspected of being a special plea, a concoction and unaesthetic. On its second time around its humanity emerged and it could be enjoyed as drama.

For a long time I had not permitted a second New York production of *A View from the Bridge* principally because I had no desire to see it through the mill a second time. However, a year or so after its first production it was done with great success in London and then in Paris, where it ran two years. It is done everywhere in this country without any apparent difficulty in reaching the emotions of the audience. This play, however, unlike *The Crucible*, I have revised, and it was the revision which London and Paris saw. The nature of the revisions bears directly upon the questions of form and style which interest students and theater workers.

The original play produced on Broadway (Viking, 1955) was in one act. It was a hard, telegraphic, unadorned drama. Nothing was permitted which did not advance the progress of Eddie's catastrophe in a most direct way. In a Note to the published play, I wrote: "What struck me first about this tale when I heard it one night in my neighborhood was how directly, with what breathtaking simplicity, it did evolve. It seemed to me, finally, that its very bareness, its absolutely unswerving path, its exposed skeleton, so to speak, was its wisdom and even its charm and must not be tampered with. . . . These *qualities* of the events themselves, their texture, seemed to me more psychologically telling than a conventional investigation in width which would necessarily relax that clear, clean line of his catastrophe."

The explanation for this point of view lies in great part in the atmosphere of the time in which the play was written. It seemed to me then that the theater was retreating into an area of psycho-sexual romanticism, and this at the very moment when great events both at home and abroad cried out for recognition and analytic inspection. In a word, I was tired of mere sympathy in the theater. The spectacle of still another misunderstood victim left me impatient. The tender emotions, I felt, were being overworked. I wanted to write in a way that would call up the faculties of knowing as well as feeling. To bathe the audience in tears, to grip people by the age-old methods of suspense, to theatricalize life, in a word, seemed faintly absurd to me if not disgusting.

In *The Crucible* I had taken a step, I felt, toward a more self-aware drama. The Puritan not only felt, but constantly referred his feelings to concepts, to codes and ideas of social and ethical importance. Feeling, it seemed to me, had to be made of importance; the dramatic victory had to be more than a triumph over the audience's indifference. It must call up a concept, a new awareness.

I had known the story of *A View from the Bridge* for a long time. A water-front worker who had known Eddie's prototype told it to me. I had never thought to make a play of it because it was too complete, there was nothing I could add. And then a time came when its very completeness became appealing. It suddenly seemed to me that I ought to deliver it onto the stage as fact; that interpretation was inherent in the very existence of the tale in the first place. I saw that the reason I had not written it was that as a whole its meaning escaped me. I could not fit it into myself. It existed apart from me and seemed not to express anything within me. Yet it refused to disappear.

I wrote it in a mood of experiment—to see what it might mean. I kept to the *tale*, trying not to change its original shape. I wanted the audience to feel toward it as I had on hearing it for the first time—not so much with heart-wringing sympathy as with wonder. For when it was told to me I knew its ending a few minutes after the teller had begun to speak. I wanted to create suspense but not by withholding information. It must be suspenseful because one knew too well how it would come out, so that the basic feeling would be the desire to stop this man and tell him what he was really doing to his life. Thus, by knowing more than the hero, the audience would rather automatically see his life through conceptualized feelings.

As a consequence of this viewpoint, the characters were not permitted to talk about this and that before getting down to their functions in the tale; when a character entered he proceeded directly to serve the catastrophe. Thus, normal naturalistic acting techniques had to be modified. Excessive and arbitrary gestures were eliminated; the set itself was shorn of every adornment. An atmosphere was attempted in which nothing existed but the purpose of the tale.

The trouble was that neither the director, the actors, nor I had had any experience with this kind of staging. It was difficult to know how far to go. We were all aware that a strange style was called for which we were unsure how to provide.

About a year later in London new conditions created new solutions. Seemingly inconsequential details suggested these solutions at times. For one, the British actors could not reproduce the Brooklyn argot and had to create one that was never heard on heaven or earth. Already naturalism was evaporated by this much: the characters were slightly strange beings in a world of their own. Also, the pay scales of the London theater made it possible to do what I could not do in New York—hire a crowd.

These seemingly mundane facts had important consequences.

The mind of Eddie Carbone is not comprehensible apart from its relation to his neighborhood, his fellow workers, his social situation. His self-esteem depends upon their estimate of him, and his value is created largely by his fidelity to the code of his culture. In New York we could have only four strategically placed actors to represent the community. In London there were at least twenty men and women surrounding the main action. Peter Brook, the British director, could then proceed to design a set which soared to the roof with fire escapes, passageways, suggested apartments, so that one sensed that Eddie was living out his horror in the midst of a certain normality, and that, invisibly and without having to speak of it, he was getting ready to invoke upon himself the wrath of his tribe. A certain size accrued to him as a result. The importance of his interior psychological dilemma was magnified to the size it would have in life. What had seemed like a mere aberration had now risen to a fatal violation of an ancient law. By the presence of his neighbors alone the play and Eddie were made more humanly understandable and moving. There was also the fact that the British cast, accustomed to playing Shakespeare, could incorporate into a seemingly realistic style the conception of the play—they moved easily into the larger-than-life attitude which the play demanded, and without the self-conscious awkwardness, the uncertain stylishness which hounds many actors without classic training.

As a consequence of not having to work at making the play seem as factual, as bare as I had conceived it, I felt now that it could afford to include elements of simple human motivation which I had rigorously excluded before—specifically, the viewpoint of Eddie's wife, and *her* dilemma in relation to him. This, in fact, accounts for almost all the added material which made it necessary to break the play in the middle for an intermission. In other words, once Eddie had been placed squarely in his social context, among his people, the mythlike feeling of the story emerged of itself, and he could be made more human and less a figure, a force. It thus seemed quite in keeping that certain details of realism should be allowed; a Christmas tree and decorations in the living room, for one, and a realistic make-up, which had been avoided in New York, where the actor was always much cleaner than a longshoreman ever is. In a word, the nature of the British actor and of the production there made it possible to concentrate more upon realistic characterization while the universality of Eddie's type was strengthened at the same time.

But it was not only external additions, such as a new kind of actor, sets, and so forth, which led to the expansion of the play. As I have said, the original was written in the hope that I would understand what it meant to me. It was only during the latter part of its run in New York that, while watching a performance one afternoon, I saw my own involvement in this story. Quite suddenly the play seemed to be "mine" and not merely a story I had heard. The revisions subsequently made were in part the result of that new awareness.

In general, then, I think it can be said that by the addition of significant psychological and behavioral detail the play became not only more human, warmer and less remote, but also a clearer statement. Eddie is still not a man to weep over; the play does not attempt to swamp an audience in tears. But it is more possible now to relate his actions to our own and thus to understand ourselves a little better not only as isolated psychological entities, but as we connect to our fellows and our long past together.

ARTHUR MILLER

A *View from the Bridge* was first presented at the New Watergate Theatre Club in London on October 11, 1956, with the following cast:

LOUIS	Richard Harris
MIKE	Norman Mitchell
ALFIERI	Michael Gwynn
EDDIE	Anthony Quayle
CATHERINE	Mary Ure
BEATRICE	Megs Jenkins
MARCO	Ian Bannen
TONY	Ralph Nossek
RODOLPHO	Brian Bedford
FIRST IMMIGRATION OFFICER	John Stone
SECOND IMMIGRATION OFFICER	Colin Rix
MR. LIPARI	Mervyn Blake
MRS. LIPARI	Catherine Willmer
A "SUBMARINE"	Peter James

The production was directed and designed by Peter Brook.
The action takes place in and around a
Tenement House in Brooklyn.

A View from
the Bridge

ACT ONE

The street and house front of a tenement building. The front is skeletal entirely. The main acting area is the living room—dining room of EDDIE's *apartment. It is a worker's flat, clean, sparse, homely. There is a rocker down front; a round dining table at center, with chairs; and a portable phonograph.*

At back are a bedroom door and an opening to the kitchen; none of these interiors are seen.

At the right, forestage, a desk. This is Mr. ALFIERI's *law office.*

There is also a telephone booth. This is not used until the last scenes, so it may be covered or left in view.

A stairway leads up to the apartment, and then farther up to the next story, which is not seen.

Ramps, representing the street, run upstage and off to right and left.

As the curtain rises, LOUIS *and* MIKE, *longshoremen, are pitching coins against the building at left.*

A distant foghorn blows.

Enter ALFIERI, *a lawyer in his fifties turning gray; he is portly, good-humored, and thoughtful. The two pitchers nod to him as he passes. He crosses the stage to his desk, removes his hat, runs his fingers through his hair, and grinning, speaks to the audience.*

ALFIERI: You wouldn't have known it, but something amusing has just happened. You see how uneasily they nod to me? That's because I am a lawyer. In this neighborhood to meet a lawyer or a priest on the street is unlucky. We're only thought of in connection with disasters, and they'd rather not get too close.

I often think that behind that suspicious little nod of theirs lie three thousand years of distrust. A lawyer means the law, and in Sicily, from where their fathers came, the law has not been a friendly idea since the Greeks were beaten.

I am inclined to notice the ruins in things, perhaps because I was born in Italy. . . . I only came here when I was twenty-five. In those days, Al Capone, the greatest Carthaginian of all, was learning his trade on these pavements, and Frankie Yale himself was cut precisely in half by a machine gun on the corner of Union Street, two blocks away. Oh, there were many here who were justly shot by unjust men. Justice is very important here.

But this is Red Hook, not Sicily. This is the slum that faces the bay on the seaward side of Brooklyn Bridge. This is the gullet of New York swallowing the tonnage of the world. And now we are quite civilized, quite American. Now we settle for half, and I like it better. I no longer keep a pistol in my filing cabinet.

And my practice is entirely unromantic.

My wife has warned me, so have my friends; they tell me the people in this neighborhood lack elegance, glamour. After all, who have I dealt with in my life? Longshoremen and their wives, and fathers and grandfathers, compensation cases, evictions, family squabbles—the petty troubles of the poor—and yet . . . every few years there is still a case, and as the parties tell me what the trouble is, the flat air in my office suddenly washes in with the green scent of the sea, the dust in this air is blown away and the thought comes that in some Caesar's year, in Calabria perhaps or on the cliff at Syracuse, another lawyer, quite differently dressed, heard the same complaint and set there as powerless as I, and watched it run its bloody course.

EDDIE *has appeared and has been pitching coins with the* *men and is highlighted among them. He is forty—a husky,* *slightly overweight longshoreman.*

This one's name was Eddie Carbone, a longshoreman working the docks from Brooklyn Bridge to the breakwater where the open sea begins.

ALFIERI *walks into darkness.*

EDDIE, *moving up steps into doorway:* Well, I'll see ya, fellas.

CATHERINE *enters from kitchen, crosses down to window, looks out.*

LOUIS: You workin' tomorrow?

EDDIE: Yeah, there's another day yet on that ship. See ya, Louis.

EDDIE *goes into the house, as light rises in the apartment.*
   CATHERINE *is waving to* LOUIS *from the window and turns to him.*

CATHERINE: Hi, Eddie!

EDDIE *is pleased and therefore shy about it; he hangs up his cap and jacket.*

EDDIE: Where you goin' all dressed up?

CATHERINE, *running her hands over her skirt:* I just got it. You like it?

EDDIE: Yeah, it's nice. And what happened to your hair?

CATHERINE: You like it? I fixed it different. *Calling to kitchen:* He's here, B.!

EDDIE: Beautiful. Turn around, lemme see in the back. *She turns for him.* Oh, if your mother was alive to see you now! She wouldn't believe it.

CATHERINE: You like it, huh?

EDDIE: You look like one of them girls that went to college. Where you goin'?

CATHERINE, *taking his arm:* Wait'll B. comes in, I'll tell you something. Here, sit down. *She is walking him to the armchair. Calling offstage:* Hurry up, will you, B.?

EDDIE, *sitting:* What's goin' on?

CATHERINE: I'll get you a beer, all right?

EDDIE: Well, tell me what happened. Come over here, talk to me.

CATHERINE: I want to wait till B. comes in. *She sits on her heels beside him.* Guess how much we paid for the skirt.

EDDIE: I think it's too short, ain't it?

CATHERINE, *standing:* No! Not when I stand up.

EDDIE: Yeah, but you gotta sit down sometimes.

CATHERINE: Eddie, it's the style now. *She walks to show him.* I mean, if you see me walkin' down the street—

EDDIE: Listen, you been givin' me the willies the way you walk down the street, I mean it.

CATHERINE: Why?

EDDIE: Catherine, I don't want to be a pest, but I'm tellin' you you're walkin' wavy.

CATHERINE: I'm walkin' wavy?

EDDIE: Now don't aggravate me, Katie, you are walkin' wavy! I don't like the looks they're givin' you in the candy store. And with them new high heels on the sidewalk— clack, clack, clack. The heads are turnin' like windmills.

CATHERINE: But those guys look at all the girls, you know that.

EDDIE: You ain't "all the girls."

CATHERINE, *almost in tears because he disapproves:* What do you want me to do? You want me to—

EDDIE: Now don't get mad, kid.

CATHERINE: Well, I don't know what you want from me.

EDDIE: Katie, I promised your mother on her deathbed. I'm responsible for you. You're a baby, you don't understand these things. I mean like when you stand here by the window, wavin' outside.

CATHERINE: I was wavin' to Louis!

EDDIE: Listen, I could tell you things about Louis which you wouldn't wave to him no more.

CATHERINE, *trying to joke him out of his warning:* Eddie, I wish there was one guy you couldn't tell me things about!

EDDIE: Catherine, do me a favor, will you? You're gettin' to be a big girl now, you gotta keep yourself more, you can't be so friendly, kid. *Calls:* Hey, B., what're you doin' in there? *To Catherine:* Get her in here, will you? I got news for her.

CATHERINE, *starting out:* What?

EDDIE: Her cousins landed.

CATHERINE, *clapping her hands together:* No! *She turns instantly and starts for the kitchen.* B.! Your cousins!

BEATRICE *enters, wiping her hands with a towel.*

BEATRICE, *in the face of Catherine's shout:* What?

CATHERINE: Your cousins got in!

BEATRICE, *astounded, turns to Eddie:* What are you talkin' about? Where?

EDDIE: I was just knockin' off work before and Tony Bereli come over to me; he says the ship is in the North River.

BEATRICE—*her hands are clasped at her breast; she seems half in fear, half in unutterable joy:* They're all right?

EDDIE: He didn't see them yet, they're still on board. But as soon as they get off he'll meet them. He figures about ten o'clock they'll be here.

BEATRICE *sits, almost weak from tension:* And they'll let them off the ship all right? That's fixed, heh?

EDDIE: Sure, they give them regular seamen papers and they walk off with the crew. Don't worry about it, B., there's nothin' to it. Couple of hours they'll be here.

BEATRICE: What happened? They wasn't supposed to be till next Thursday.

EDDIE: I don't know; they put them on any ship they can get them out on. Maybe the other ship they was supposed to take there was some danger— What you cryin' about?

BEATRICE, *astounded and afraid:* I'm— I just—I can't believe it! I didn't even buy a new tablecloth; I was gonna wash the walls—

EDDIE: Listen, they'll think it's a millionaire's house compared to the way they live. Don't worry about the walls. They'll be thankful. *To Catherine:* Whyn't you run down buy a tablecloth. Go ahead, here. *He is reaching into his pocket.*

CATHERINE: There's no stores open now.

EDDIE, *to Beatrice:* You was gonna put a new cover on the chair.

BEATRICE: I know—well, I thought it was gonna be next

week! I was gonna clean the walls, I was gonna wax the floors. *She stands disturbed.*

CATHERINE, *pointing upward:* Maybe Mrs. Dondero upstairs—

BEATRICE, *of the tablecloth:* No, hers is worse than this one. *Suddenly:* My God, I don't even have nothin' to eat for them! *She starts for the kitchen.*

EDDIE, *reaching out and grabbing her arm:* Hey, hey! Take it easy.

BEATRICE: No, I'm just nervous, that's all. *To Catherine:* I'll make the fish.

EDDIE: You're savin' their lives, what're you worryin' about the tablecloth? They probably didn't see a tablecloth in their whole life where they come from.

BEATRICE, *looking into his eyes:* I'm just worried about you, that's all. I'm worried.

EDDIE: Listen, as long as they know where they're gonna sleep.

BEATRICE: I told them in the letters. They're sleepin' on the floor.

EDDIE: Beatrice, all I'm worried about is you got such a heart that I'll end up on the floor with you, and they'll be in our bed.

BEATRICE: All right, stop it.

EDDIE: Because as soon as you see a tired relative, I end up on the floor.

BEATRICE: When did you end up on the floor?

EDDIE: When your father's house burned down I didn't end up on the floor?

BEATRICE: Well, their house burned down!

EDDIE: Yeah, but it didn't keep burnin' for two weeks!

BEATRICE: All right, look, I'll tell them to go someplace else.

She starts into the kitchen.

EDDIE: Now wait a minute. Beatrice! *She halts. He goes to her.* I just don't want you bein' pushed around, that's all. You got too big a heart. *He touches her hand.* What're you so touchy?

BEATRICE: I'm just afraid if it don't turn out good you'll be mad at me.

EDDIE: Listen, if everybody keeps his mouth shut, nothin' can happen. They'll pay for their board.

BEATRICE: Oh, I told them.

EDDIE: Then what the hell. *Pause. He moves.* It's an honor, B. I mean it. I was just thinkin' before, comin' home, suppose my father didn't come to this country, and I was starvin' like them over there . . . and I had people in America could keep me a couple of months? The man would be honored to lend me a place to sleep.

BEATRICE—*there are tears in her eyes. She turns to Catherine:* You see what he is? *She turns and grabs Eddie's face in her hands.* Mmm! You're an angel! God'll bless you. *He is gratefully smiling.* You'll see, you'll get a blessing for this!

EDDIE, *laughing:* I'll settle for my own bed.

BEATRICE: Go, Baby, set the table.

CATHERINE: We didn't tell him about me yet.

BEATRICE: Let him eat first, then we'll tell him. Bring everything in. *She hurries Catherine out.*

EDDIE, *sitting at the table:* What's all that about? Where's she goin'?

BEATRICE: Noplace. It's very good news, Eddie. I want you to be happy.

EDDIE: What's goin' on?

CATHERINE *enters with plates, forks.*

BEATRICE: She's got a job.

Pause. EDDIE *looks at* CATHERINE, *then back to* BEATRICE.

EDDIE: What job? She's gonna finish school.

CATHERINE: Eddie, you won't believe it—

EDDIE: No—no, you gonna finish school. What kinda job, what do you mean? All of a sudden you—

CATHERINE: Listen a minute, it's wonderful.

EDDIE: It's not wonderful. You'll never get nowheres unless you finish school. You can't take no job. Why didn't you ask me before you take a job?

BEATRICE: She's askin' you now, she didn't take nothin' yet.

CATHERINE: Listen a minute! I came to school this morning and the principal called me out of the class, see? To go to his office.

EDDIE: Yeah?

CATHERINE: So I went in and he says to me he's got my records, y'know? And there's a company wants a girl right away. It ain't exactly a secretary, it's a stenographer first, but pretty soon you get to be secretary. And he says to me that I'm the best student in the whole class—

BEATRICE: You hear that?

EDDIE: Well why not? Sure she's the best.

CATHERINE: I'm the best student, he says, and if I want, I should take the job and the end of the year he'll let me take the examination and he'll give me the certificate. So I'll save practically a year!

EDDIE, *strangely nervous:* Where's the job? What company?

CATHERINE: It's a big plumbing company over Nostrand Avenue.

EDDIE: Nostrand Avenue and where?

CATHERINE: It's someplace by the Navy Yard.

BEATRICE: Fifty dollars a week, Eddie.

EDDIE, *to Catherine, surprised:* Fifty?

CATHERINE: I swear.

Pause.

EDDIE: What about all the stuff you wouldn't learn this year, though?

CATHERINE: There's nothin' more to learn, Eddie, I just gotta practice from now on. I know all the symbols and I know the keyboard. I'll just get faster, that's all. And when I'm workin' I'll keep gettin' better and better, you see?

BEATRICE: Work is the best practice anyway.

EDDIE: That ain't what I wanted, though.

CATHERINE: Why! It's a great big company—

EDDIE: I don't like that neighborhood over there.

CATHERINE: It's a block and a half from the subway, he says.

EDDIE: Near the Navy Yard plenty can happen in a block and a half. And a plumbin' company! That's one step over the water front. They're practically longshoremen.

BEATRICE: Yeah, but she'll be in the office, Eddie.

EDDIE: I know she'll be in the office, but that ain't what I had in mind.

BEATRICE: Listen, she's gotta go to work sometime.

EDDIE: Listen, B., she'll be with a lotta plumbers? And sailors up and down the street? So what did she go to school for?

CATHERINE: But it's fifty a week, Eddie.

EDDIE: Look, did I ask you for money? I supported you this long I support you a little more. Please, do me a favor, will ya? I want you to be with different kind of people. I want you to be in a nice office. Maybe a lawyer's office someplace in New York in one of them nice buildings. I mean if you're gonna get outa here then get out; don't go practically in the same kind of neighborhood.

Pause. CATHERINE *lowers her eyes.*

BEATRICE: Go, Baby, bring in the supper. *Catherine goes out.* Think about it a little bit, Eddie. Please. She's crazy to start work. It's not a little shop, it's a big company. Some day she could be a secretary. They picked her out of the whole class. *He is silent, staring down at the tablecloth, fingering the pattern.* What are you worried about? She could take care of herself. She'll get out of the subway and be in the office in two minutes.

EDDIE, *somehow sickened:* I know that neighborhood, B., I don't like it.

BEATRICE: Listen, if nothin' happened to her in this neighborhood it ain't gonna happen noplace else. *She turns his face to her.* Look, you gotta get used to it, she's no baby no more. Tell her to take it. *He turns his head away.* You hear me? *She is angering.* I don't understand you; she's seventeen years old, you gonna keep her in the house all her life?

EDDIE, *insulted:* What kinda remark is that?

BEATRICE, *with sympathy but insistent force:* Well, I don't understand when it ends. First it was gonna be when she graduated high school, so she graduated high school. Then it was gonna be when she learned stenographer, so she learned stenographer. So what're we gonna wait for now? I mean it, Eddie, sometimes I don't understand you; they picked her out of the whole class, it's an honor for her.

CATHERINE *enters with food, which she silently sets on the table. After a moment of watching her face,* EDDIE *breaks into a smile, but it almost seems that tears will form in his eyes.*

EDDIE: With your hair that way you look like a madonna, you know that? You're the madonna type. *She doesn't look at him, but continues ladling out food onto the plates.* You wanna go to work, heh, Madonna?

CATHERINE, *softly:* Yeah.

EDDIE, *with a sense of her childhood, her babyhood, and the years:* All right, go to work. *She looks at him, then rushes and hugs him.* Hey, hey! Take it easy! *He holds her face away from him to look at her.* What're you cryin' about? *He is affected by her, but smiles his emotion away.*

CATHERINE, *sitting at her place:* I just— *Bursting out:* I'm gonna buy all new dishes with my first pay! *They laugh warmly.* I mean it. I'll fix up the whole house! I'll buy a rug!

EDDIE: And then you'll move away.

CATHERINE: No, Eddie!

EDDIE, *grinning:* Why not? That's life. And you'll come visit on Sundays, then once a month, then Christmas and New Year's, finally.

CATHERINE, *grasping his arm to reassure him and to erase the accusation:* No, please!

EDDIE, *smiling but hurt:* I only ask you one thing—don't trust nobody. You got a good aunt but she's got too big a heart, you learned bad from her. Believe me.

BEATRICE: Be the way you are, Katie, don't listen to him.

EDDIE, *to Beatrice—strangely and quickly resentful:* You lived in a house all your life, what do you know about it? You never worked in your life.

BEATRICE: She likes people. What's wrong with that?

EDDIE: Because most people ain't people. She's goin' to work; plumbers; they'll chew her to pieces if she don't watch out. *To Catherine:* Believe me, Katie, the less you trust, the less you be sorry.

EDDIE *crosses himself and the women do the same, and they eat.*

CATHERINE: First thing I'll buy is a rug, heh, B.?

BEATRICE: I don't mind. *To Eddie:* I smelled coffee all day today. You unloadin' coffee today?

EDDIE: Yeah, a Brazil ship.

CATHERINE: I smelled it too. It smelled all over the neighborhood.

EDDIE: That's one time, boy, to be a longshoreman is a pleasure. I could work coffee ships twenty hours a day. You go down in the hold, y'know? It's like flowers, that smell. We'll bust a bag tomorrow, I'll bring you some.

BEATRICE: Just be sure there's no spiders in it, will ya? I mean it. *She directs this to Catherine, rolling her eyes upward.* I still remember that spider coming out of that bag he brung home. I nearly died.

EDDIE: You call that a spider? You oughta see what comes outa the bananas sometimes.

BEATRICE: Don't talk about it!

EDDIE: I seen spiders could stop a Buick.

BEATRICE, *clapping her hands over her ears:* All right, shut up!

EDDIE, *laughing and taking a watch out of his pocket:* Well, who started with spiders?

BEATRICE: All right, I'm sorry, I didn't mean it. Just don't bring none home again. What time is it?

EDDIE: Quarter nine. *Puts watch back in his pocket. They continue eating in silence.*

CATHERINE: He's bringin' them ten o'clock, Tony?

EDDIE: Around, yeah. *He eats.*

CATHERINE: Eddie, suppose somebody asks if they're livin' here. *He looks at her as though already she had divulged something publicly. Defensively:* I mean if they ask.

EDDIE: Now look, Baby, I can see we're gettin' mixed up again here.

CATHERINE: No, I just mean . . . people'll see them goin' in and out.

EDDIE: I don't care who sees them goin' in and out as long as you don't see them goin' in and out. And this goes for you too, B. You don't see nothin' and you don't know nothin'.

BEATRICE: What do you mean? I understand.

EDDIE: You don't understand; you still think you can talk about this to somebody just a little bit. Now lemme say it once and for all, because you're makin' me nervous again, both of you. I don't care if somebody comes in the house and sees them sleepin' on the floor, it never comes out of your mouth who they are or what they're doin' here.

BEATRICE: Yeah, but my mother'll know—

EDDIE: Sure she'll know, but just don't you be the one who told her, that's all. This is the United States government you're playin' with now, this is the Immigration Bureau. If you said it you knew it, if you didn't say it you didn't know it.

CATHERINE: Yeah, but Eddie, suppose somebody—

EDDIE: I don't care what question it is. You—don't—know—nothin'. They got stool pigeons all over this neighborhood they're payin' them every week for information, and you don't know who they are. It could be your best friend. You hear? *To Beatrice:* Like Vinny Bolzano, remember Vinny?

BEATRICE: Oh, yeah. God forbid.

EDDIE: Tell her about Vinny. *To Catherine:* You think I'm blowin' steam here? *To Beatrice:* Go ahead, tell her. *To Catherine:* You was a baby then. There was a family lived next door to her mother, he was about sixteen—

BEATRICE: No, he was no more than fourteen, cause I was to

his confirmation in Saint Agnes. But the family had an uncle that they were hidin' in the house, and he snitched to the Immigration.

CATHERINE: The kid snitched?

EDDIE: On his own uncle!

CATHERINE: What, was he crazy?

EDDIE: He was crazy after, I tell you that, boy.

BEATRICE: Oh, it was terrible. He had five brothers and the old father. And they grabbed him in the kitchen and pulled him down the stairs—three flights his head was bouncin' like a coconut. And they spit on him in the street, his own father and his brothers. The whole neighborhood was cryin'.

CATHERINE: Ts! So what happened to him?

BEATRICE: I think he went away. *To Eddie:* I never seen him again, did you?

EDDIE *rises during this, taking out his watch:* Him? You'll never see him no more, a guy do a thing like that? How's he gonna show his face? *To Catherine, as he gets up uneasily:* Just remember, kid, you can quicker get back a million dollars that was stole than a word that you gave away. *He is standing now, stretching his back.*

CATHERINE: Okay, I won't say a word to nobody, I swear.

EDDIE: Gonna rain tomorrow. We'll be slidin' all over the decks. Maybe you oughta put something on for them, they be here soon.

BEATRICE: I only got fish, I hate to spoil it if they ate already. I'll wait, it only takes a few minutes; I could broil it.

CATHERINE: What happens, Eddie, when that ship pulls out and they ain't on it, though? Don't the captain say nothin'?

EDDIE, *slicing an apple with his pocket knife:* Captain's pieced off, what do you mean?

CATHERINE: Even the captain?

EDDIE: What's the matter, the captain don't have to live? Captain gets a piece, maybe one of the mates, piece for the guy in Italy who fixed the papers for them, Tony here'll get a little bite. . . .

BEATRICE: I just hope they get work here, that's all I hope.

EDDIE: Oh, the syndicate'll fix jobs for them; till they pay 'em off they'll get them work every day. It's after the pay-off, then they'll have to scramble like the rest of us.

BEATRICE: Well, it be better than they got there.

EDDIE: Oh sure, well, listen. So you gonna start Monday, heh, Madonna?

CATHERINE, *embarrassed:* I'm supposed to, yeah.

EDDIE *is standing facing the two seated women. First* BEATRICE *smiles, then* CATHERINE, *for a powerful emotion is on him, a childish one and a knowing fear, and the tears show in his eyes—and they are shy before the avowal.*

EDDIE, *sadly smiling, yet somehow proud of her:* Well . . . I hope you have good luck. I wish you the best. You know that, kid.

CATHERINE, *rising, trying to laugh:* You sound like I'm goin' a million miles!

EDDIE: I know. I guess I just never figured on one thing.

CATHERINE, *smiling:* What?

EDDIE: That you would ever grow up. *He utters a soundless laugh at himself, feeling his breast pocket of his shirt.* I left a cigar in my other coat, I think. *He starts for the bedroom.*

CATHERINE: Stay there! I'll get it for you.

She hurries out. There is a slight pause, and EDDIE *turns to* BEATRICE, *who has been avoiding his gaze.*

EDDIE: What are you mad at me lately?

BEATRICE: Who's mad? *She gets up, clearing the dishes.* I'm not mad. *She picks up the dishes and turns to him.* You're the one is mad. *She turns and goes into the kitchen as Catherine enters from the bedroom with a cigar and a pack of matches.*

CATHERINE: Here! I'll light it for you! *She strikes a match and holds it to his cigar. He puffs. Quietly:* Don't worry about me, Eddie, heh?

EDDIE: Don't burn yourself. *Just in time she blows out the match.* You better go in help her with the dishes.

CATHERINE *turns quickly to the table, and, seeing the table cleared, she says, almost guiltily:* Oh! *She hurries into the kitchen, and as she exits there:* I'll do the dishes, B.!

Alone, EDDIE *stands looking toward the kitchen for a moment. Then he takes out his watch, glances at it, replaces it in his pocket, sits in the armchair, and stares at the smoke flowing out of his mouth.*

The lights go down, then come up on ALFIERI, *who has moved onto the forestage.*

ALFIERI: He was as good a man as he had to be in a life that was hard and even. He worked on the piers when there was work, he brought home his pay, and he lived. And toward ten o'clock of that night, after they had eaten, the cousins came.

The lights fade on ALFIERI *and rise on the street.*

Enter TONY, *escorting* MARCO *and* RODOLPHO, *each with a valise.* TONY *halts, indicates the house. They stand for a moment looking at it.*

MARCO—*he is a square-built peasant of thirty-two, suspicious, tender, and quiet-voiced:* Thank you.

TONY: You're on your own now. Just be careful, that's all. Ground floor.

MARCO: Thank you.

TONY, *indicating the house:* I'll see you on the pier tomorrow. You'll go to work.

MARCO *nods.* TONY *continues on walking down the street.*

RODOLPHO: This will be the first house I ever walked into in America! Imagine! She said they were poor!

MARCO: Ssh! Come. *They go to door.*

MARCO *knocks. The lights rise in the room.* EDDIE *goes and opens the door. Enter* MARCO *and* RODOLPHO, *removing their caps.* BEATRICE *and* CATHERINE *enter from the kitchen. The lights fade in the street.*

EDDIE: You Marco?

MARCO: Marco.

EDDIE: Come on in! *He shakes Marco's hand.*

BEATRICE: Here, take the bags!

MARCO *nods, looks to the women and fixes on Beatrice. Crosses to Beatrice:* Are you my cousin?

> *She nods. He kisses her hand.*

BEATRICE, *above the table, touching her chest with her hand:* Beatrice. This is my husband, Eddie. *All nod.* Catherine, my sister Nancy's daughter. *The brothers nod.*

MARCO, *indicating Rodolpho:* My brother. Rodolpho. *Rodolpho nods. Marco comes with a certain formal stiffness to Eddie.* I want to tell you now Eddie—when you say go, we will go.

EDDIE: Oh, no . . . *Takes Marco's bag.*

MARCO: I see it's a small house, but soon, maybe, we can have our own house.

EDDIE: You're welcome, Marco, we got plenty of room here. Katie, give them supper, heh? *Exits into bedroom with their bags.*

CATHERINE: Come here, sit down. I'll get you some soup.

MARCO, *as they go to the table:* We ate on the ship. Thank you. *To Eddie, calling off to bedroom:* Thank you.

BEATRICE: Get some coffee. We'll all have coffee. Come sit down.

> RODOLPHO *and* MARCO *sit, at the table.*

CATHERINE, *wondrously:* How come he's so dark and you're so light, Rodolpho?

RODOLPHO, *ready to laugh:* I don't know. A thousand years ago, they say, the Danes invaded Sicily.

> BEATRICE *kisses* RODOLPHO. *They laugh as* EDDIE *enters.*

CATHERINE, *to Beatrice:* He's practically blond!

EDDIE: How's the coffee doin'?

CATHERINE, *brought up:* I'm gettin' it. *She hurries out to kitchen.*

EDDIE *sits on his rocker:* Yiz have a nice trip?

MARCO: The ocean is always rough. But we are good sailors.

EDDIE: No trouble gettin' here?

MARCO: No. The man brought us. Very nice man.

RODOLPHO, *to Eddie:* He says we start to work tomorrow. Is he honest?

EDDIE, *laughing:* No. But as long as you owe them money, they'll get you plenty of work. *To Marco:* Yiz ever work on the piers in Italy?

MARCO: Piers? Ts!—no.

RODOLPHO, *smiling at the smallness of his town:* In our town there are no piers, only the beach, and little fishing boats.

BEATRICE: So what kinda work did yiz do?

MARCO, *shrugging shyly, even embarrassed:* Whatever there is, anything.

RODOLPHO: Sometimes they build a house, or if they fix the bridge—Marco is a mason and I bring him the cement. *He laughs.* In harvest time we work in the fields . . . if there is work. Anything.

EDDIE: Still bad there, heh?

MARCO: Bad, yes.

RODOLPHO, *laughing:* It's terrible! We stand around all day in the piazza listening to the fountain like birds. Everybody waits only for the train.

BEATRICE: What's on the train?

RODOLPHO: Nothing. But if there are many passengers and you're lucky you make a few lire to push the taxi up the hill.

Enter CATHERINE; *she listens.*

BEATRICE: You gotta push a taxi?

RODOLPHO, *laughing:* Oh, sure! It's a feature in our town. The horses in our town are skinnier than goats. So if there are too many passengers we help to push the carriages up to the hotel. *He laughs.* In our town the horses are only for show.

CATHERINE: Why don't they have automobile taxis?

RODOLPHO: There is one. We push that too. *They laugh.* Everything in our town, you gotta push!

BEATRICE, *to Eddie:* How do you like that!

EDDIE, *to Marco:* So what're you wanna do, you gonna stay here in this country or you wanna go back?

MARCO, *surprised:* Go back?

EDDIE: Well, you're married, ain't you?

MARCO: Yes. I have three children.

BEATRICE: Three! I thought only one.

MARCO: Oh, no. I have three now. Four years, five years, six years.

BEATRICE: Ah . . . I bet they're cryin' for you already, heh?

MARCO: What can I do? The older one is sick in his chest. My wife—she feeds them from her own mouth. I tell you the truth, if I stay there they will never grow up. They eat the sunshine.

BEATRICE: My God. So how long you want to stay?

MARCO: With your permission, we will stay maybe a—

EDDIE: She don't mean in this house, she means in the country.

MARCO: Oh. Maybe four, five, six years, I think.

RODOLPHO, *smiling:* He trusts his wife.

BEATRICE: Yeah, but maybe you'll get enough, you'll be able to go back quicker.

MARCO: I hope. I don't know. *To Eddie:* I understand it's not so good here either.

EDDIE: Oh, you guys'll be all right—till you pay them off, anyway. After that, you'll have to scramble, that's all. But you'll make better here than you could there.

RODOLPHO: How much? We hear all kinds of figures. How much can a man make? We work hard, we'll work all day, all night—

MARCO *raises a hand to hush him.*

EDDIE—*he is coming more and more to address Marco only:* On the average a whole year? Maybe—well, it's hard to say, see. Sometimes we lay off, there's no ships three four weeks.

MARCO: Three, four weeks!—Ts!

EDDIE: But I think you could probably—thirty, forty a week, over the whole twelve months of the year.

MARCO, *rises, crosses to Eddie:* Dollars.

EDDIE: Sure dollars.

MARCO *puts an arm round* RODOLPHO *and they laugh.*

MARCO: If we can stay here a few months, Beatrice—

BEATRICE: Listen, you're welcome, Marco

MARCO: Because I could send them a little more if I stay here.

BEATRICE: As long as you want, we got plenty a room.

MARCO, *his eyes are showing tears:* My wife— *To Eddie:* My wife—I want to send right away maybe twenty dollars—

EDDIE: You could send them something next week already.

MARCO—*he is near tears:* Eduardo . . . *He goes to Eddie, offering his hand.*

EDDIE: Don't thank me. Listen, what the hell, it's no skin off me. *To Catherine:* What happened to the coffee?

CATHERINE: I got it on. *To Rodolpho:* You married too? No.

RODOLPHO *rises:* Oh, no . . .

BEATRICE, *to Catherine:* I told you he—

CATHERINE: I know, I just thought maybe he got married recently.

RODOLPHO: I have no money to get married. I have a nice face, but no money. *He laughs.*

CATHERINE, *to Beatrice:* He's a real blond!

BEATRICE, *to Rodolpho:* You want to stay here too, heh? For good?

RODOLPHO: Me? Yes, forever! Me, I want to be an American. And then I want to go back to Italy when I am rich, and I will buy a motorcycle. *He smiles. Marco shakes him affectionately.*

CATHERINE: A motorcycle!

RODOLPHO: With a motorcycle in Italy you will never starve any more.

BEATRICE: I'll get you coffee. *She exits to the kitchen.*

EDDIE: What you do with a motorcycle?

MARCO: He dreams, he dreams.

RODOLPHO, *to Marco:* Why? *To Eddie:* Messages! The rich people in the hotel always need someone who will carry a message. But quickly, and with a great noise. With a blue motorcycle I would station myself in the courtyard of the hotel, and in a little while I would have messages.

MARCO: When you have no wife you have dreams.

EDDIE: Why can't you just walk, or take a trolley or sump'm?

Enter BEATRICE *with coffee.*

RODOLPHO: Oh, no, the machine, the machine is necessary. A man comes into a great hotel and says, I am a messenger. Who is this man? He disappears walking, there is no noise, nothing. Maybe he will never come back, maybe he will never deliver the message. But a man who rides up on a great machine, this man is responsible, this man exists. He will be given messages. *He helps Beatrice set out the coffee things.* I am also a singer, though.

EDDIE: You mean a regular—?

RODOLPHO: Oh, yes. One night last year Andreola got sick. Baritone. And I took his place in the garden of the hotel. Three arias I sang without a mistake! Thousand-lire notes they threw from the tables, money was falling like a storm in the treasury. It was magnificent. We lived six months on that night, eh, Marco?

MARCO *nods doubtfully.*

MARCO: Two months.

EDDIE *laughs.*

BEATRICE: Can't you get a job in that place?

RODOLPHO: Andreola got better. He's a baritone, very strong.

BEATRICE *laughs.*

MARCO, *regretfully, to Beatrice:* He sang too loud.

RODOLPHO: Why too loud?

MARCO: Too loud. The guests in that hotel are all English-men. They don't like too loud.

RODOLPHO, *to Catherine:* Nobody ever said it was too loud!

MARCO: I say. It was too loud. *To Beatrice:* I knew it as soon as he started to sing. Too loud.

RODOLPHO: Then why did they throw so much money?

MARCO: They paid for your courage. The English like cour-age. But once is enough.

RODOLPHO, *to all but Marco:* I never heard anybody say it was too loud.

CATHERINE: Did you ever hear of jazz?

RODOLPHO: Oh, sure! I *sing* jazz.

CATHERINE *rises:* You could sing jazz?

RODOLPHO: Oh, I sing Napolidan, jazz, bel canto—I sing "Paper Doll," you like "Paper Doll"?

CATHERINE: Oh, sure, I'm crazy for "Paper Doll." Go ahead, sing it.

RODOLPHO *takes his stance after getting a nod of permission from* MARCO, *and with a high tenor voice begins singing:*

> I'll tell you boys it's tough to be alone,
> And it's tough to love a doll that's not your own.
> I'm through with all of them,
> I'll never fall again,
> Hey, boy, what you gonna do?
> I'm gonna buy a paper doll that I can call my own,
> A doll that other fellows cannot steal.

EDDIE *rises and moves upstage.*

> And then those flirty, flirty guys
> With their flirty, flirty eyes
> Will have to flirt with dollies that are real—

EDDIE: Hey, kid—hey, wait a minute—

CATHERINE, *enthralled:* Leave him finish, it's beautiful! *To Beatrice:* He's terrific! It's terrific, Rodolpho.

EDDIE: Look, kid; you don't want to be picked up, do ya?

MARCO: No—no! *He rises.*

EDDIE, *indicating the rest of the building:* Because we never had no singers here . . . and all of a sudden there's a singer in the house, y'know what I mean?

MARCO: Yes, yes. You'll be quiet, Rodolpho.

EDDIE—*he is flushed:* They got guys all over the place, Marco. I mean.

MARCO: Yes. He'll be quiet. *To Rodolpho:* You'll be quiet.

RODOLPHO *nods.*

EDDIE *has risen, with iron control, even a smile. He moves to* CATHERINE.

EDDIE: What's the high heels for, Garbo?

CATHERINE: I figured for tonight—

EDDIE: Do me a favor, will you? Go ahead.

Embarrassed now, angered, CATHERINE *goes out into the bedroom.* BEATRICE *watches her go and gets up; in passing, she gives* EDDIE *a cold look, restrained only by the strangers, and goes to the table to pour coffee.*

EDDIE, *striving to laugh, and to Marco, but directed as much to Beatrice:* All actresses they want to be around here.

RODOLPHO, *happy about it:* In Italy too! All the girls.

CATHERINE *emerges from the bedroom in low-heel shoes, comes to the table.* RODOLPHO *is lifting a cup.*

EDDIE—*he is sizing up Rodolpho, and there is a concealed suspicion:* Yeah, heh?

RODOLPHO: Yes! *Laughs, indicating Catherine:* Especially when they are so beautiful!

CATHERINE: You like sugar?

RODOLPHO: Sugar? Yes! I like sugar very much!

EDDIE *is downstage, watching as she pours a spoonful of sugar into his cup, his face puffed with trouble, and the room dies.*
Lights rise on ALFIERI.

ALFIERI: Who can ever know what will be discovered? Eddie Carbone had never expected to have a destiny. A man works, raises his family, goes bowling, eats, gets old, and then he dies. Now, as the weeks passed, there was a future, there was a trouble that would not go away.

The lights fade on ALFIERI, *then rise on* EDDIE *standing at the doorway of the house.* BEATRICE *enters on the street. She sees* EDDIE, *smiles at him. He looks away.*
She starts to enter the house when EDDIE *speaks.*

EDDIE: It's after eight.

BEATRICE: Well, it's a long show at the Paramount.

EDDIE: They must've seen every picture in Brooklyn by now. He's supposed to stay in the house when he ain't working. He ain't supposed to go advertising himself.

BEATRICE: Well that's his trouble, what do you care? If they pick him up they pick him up, that's all. Come in the house.

EDDIE: What happened to the stenography? I don't see her practice no more.

BEATRICE: She'll get back to it. She's excited, Eddie.

EDDIE: She tell you anything?

BEATRICE *comes to him, now the subject is opened:* What's the matter with you? He's a nice kid, what do you want from him?

EDDIE: That's a nice kid? He gives me the heeby-jeebies.

BEATRICE, *smiling:* Ah, go on, you're just jealous.

EDDIE: Of *him?* Boy, you don't think much of me.

BEATRICE: I don't understand you. What's so terrible about him?

EDDIE: You mean it's all right with you? That's gonna be her husband?

BEATRICE: Why? He's a nice fella, hard workin', he's a good-lookin' fella.

EDDIE: He sings on the ships, didja know that?

BEATRICE: What do you mean, he sings?

EDDIE: Just what I said, he sings. Right on the deck, all of a sudden, a whole song comes out of his mouth—with motions. You know what they're callin' him now? Paper Doll they're callin' him, Canary. He's like a weird. He comes out on the pier, one-two-three, it's a regular free show.

BEATRICE: Well, he's a kid; he don't know how to behave himself yet.

EDDIE: And with that wacky hair; he's like a chorus girl or sump'm.

BEATRICE: So he's blond, so—

EDDIE: I just hope that's his regular hair, that's all I hope.

BEATRICE: You crazy or sump'm? *She tries to turn him to her.*

EDDIE—*he keeps his head turned away:* What's so crazy? I don't like his whole way.

BEATRICE: Listen, you never seen a blond guy in your life? What about Whitey Balso?

EDDIE, *turning to her victoriously:* Sure, but Whitey don't sing; he don't do like that on the ships.

BEATRICE: Well, maybe that's the way they do in Italy.

EDDIE: Then why don't his brother sing? Marco goes around like a man; nobody kids Marco. *He moves from her, halts. She realizes there is a campaign solidified in him.* I tell you the truth I'm surprised I have to tell you all this. I mean I'm surprised, B.

BEATRICE—*she goes to him with purpose now:* Listen, you ain't gonna start nothin' here.

EDDIE: I ain't startin' nothin', but I ain't gonna stand around lookin' at that. For that character I didn't bring her up. I swear, B., I'm surprised at you; I sit there waitin' for you to wake up but everything is great with you.

BEATRICE: No, everything ain't great with me.

EDDIE: No?

BEATRICE: No. But I got other worries.

EDDIE: Yeah. *He is already weakening.*

BEATRICE: Yeah, you want me to tell you?

EDDIE, *in retreat:* Why? What worries you got?

BEATRICE: When am I gonna be a wife again, Eddie?

EDDIE: I ain't been feelin' good. They bother me since they came.

BEATRICE: It's almost three months you don't feel good; they're only here a couple of weeks. It's three months, Eddie.

EDDIE: I don't know, B. I don't want to talk about it.

BEATRICE: What's the matter, Eddie, you don't like me, heh?

EDDIE: What do you mean, I don't like you? I said I don't feel good, that's all.

BEATRICE: Well, tell me, am I doing something wrong? Talk to me.

EDDIE—*Pause. He can't speak, then:* I can't. I can't talk about it.

BEATRICE: Well tell me what—

EDDIE: I got nothin' to say about it!

She stands for a moment; he is looking off; she turns to go into the house.

EDDIE: I'll be all right, B.; just lay off me, will ya? I'm worried about her.

BEATRICE: The girl is gonna be eighteen years old, it's time already.

EDDIE: B., he's taking her for a ride!

BEATRICE: All right, that's her ride. What're you gonna stand over her till she's forty? Eddie, I want you to cut it out now, you hear me? I don't like it! Now come in the house.

EDDIE: I want to take a walk, I'll be in right away.

BEATRICE: They ain't goin' to come any quicker if you stand in the street. It ain't nice, Eddie.

EDDIE: I'll be in right away. Go ahead. *He walks off.*

She goes into the house. EDDIE *glances up the street, sees* LOUIS *and* MIKE *coming, and sits on an iron railing.* LOUIS *and* MIKE *enter.*

LOUIS: Wanna go bowlin' tonight?

EDDIE: I'm too tired. Goin' to sleep.

LOUIS: How's your two submarines?

EDDIE: They're okay.

LOUIS: I see they're gettin' work allatime.

EDDIE: Oh yeah, they're doin' all right.

MIKE: That's what we oughta do. We oughta leave the country and come in under the water. Then we get work.

EDDIE: You ain't kiddin'.

LOUIS: Well, what the hell. Y'know?

EDDIE: Sure.

LOUIS—*sits on railing beside Eddie:* Believe me, Eddie, you got a lotta credit comin' to you.

EDDIE: Aah, they don't bother me, don't cost me nutt'n.

MIKE: That older one, boy, he's a regular bull. I seen him the other day liftin' coffee bags over the Matson Line. They leave him alone he woulda load the whole ship by himself.

EDDIE: Yeah, he's a strong guy, that guy. Their father was a regular giant, supposed to be.

LOUIS: Yeah, you could see. He's a regular slave.

MIKE, *grinning:* That blond one, though— *Eddie looks at him.* He's got a sense of humor. *Louis snickers.*

EDDIE, *searchingly:* Yeah. He's funny—

MIKE, *starting to laugh:* Well he ain't exackly funny, but he's always like makin' remarks like, y'know? He comes around, everybody's laughin'. *Louis laughs.*

EDDIE, *uncomfortably, grinning:* Yeah, well . . . he's got a sense of humor.

MIKE, *laughing:* Yeah, I mean, he's always makin' like remarks, like, y'know?

EDDIE: Yeah, I know. But he's a kid yet, y'know? He—he's just a kid, that's all.

MIKE, *getting hysterical with Louis:* I know. You take one look at him—everybody's happy. *Louis laughs.* I worked one day with him last week over the Moore-MacCormack Line, I'm tellin' you they was all hysterical. *Louis and he explode in laughter.*

EDDIE: Why? What'd he do?

MIKE: I don't know . . . he was just humorous. You never can remember what he says, y'know? But it's the way he says it. I mean he gives you a look sometimes and you start laughin'!

EDDIE: Yeah. *Troubled:* He's got a sense of humor.

MIKE, *gasping:* Yeah.

LOUIS, *rising:* Well, we see ya, Eddie.

EDDIE: Take it easy.

LOUIS: Yeah. See ya.

MIKE: If you wanna come bowlin' later we're goin' Flatbush Avenue.

Laughing, they move to exit, meeting RODOLPHO *and* CATHERINE *entering on the street. Their laughter rises as they see* RODOLPHO, *who does not understand but joins in.* EDDIE *moves to enter the house as* LOUIS *and* MIKE *exit.* CATHERINE *stops him at the door.*

CATHERINE: Hey, Eddie—what a picture we saw! Did we laugh!

EDDIE—*he can't help smiling at sight of her:* Where'd you go?

CATHERINE: Paramount. It was with those two guys, y'know? That—

EDDIE: Brooklyn Paramount?

CATHERINE, *with an edge of anger, embarrassed before Rodolpho:* Sure, the Brooklyn Paramount. I told you we wasn't goin' to New York.

EDDIE, *retreating before the threat of her anger:* All right, I only asked you. *To Rodolpho:* I just don't want her hangin' around Times Square, see? It's full of tramps over there.

RODOLPHO: I would like to go to Broadway once, Eddie. I would like to walk with her once where the theaters are and the opera. Since I was a boy I see pictures of those lights.

EDDIE, *his little patience waning:* I want to talk to her a minute, Rodolpho. Go inside, will you?

RODOLPHO: Eddie, we only walk together in the streets. She teaches me.

CATHERINE: You know what he can't get over? That there's no fountains in Brooklyn!

EDDIE, *smiling unwillingly:* Fountains? *Rodolpho smiles at his own naïveté.*

CATHERINE: In Italy he says, every town's got fountains, and they meet there. And you know what? They got oranges on the trees where he comes from, and lemons. Imagine—on the trees? I mean it's interesting. But he's crazy for New York.

RODOLPHO, *attempting familiarity:* Eddie, why can't we go once to Broadway—?

EDDIE: Look, I gotta tell her something—

RODOLPHO: Maybe you can come too. I want to see all those lights. *He sees no response in Eddie's face. He glances at Catherine.* I'll walk by the river before I go to sleep. *He walks off down the street.*

CATHERINE: Why don't you talk to him, Eddie? He blesses you, and you don't talk to him hardly.

EDDIE, *enveloping her with his eyes:* I bless you and you don't talk to me. *He tries to smile.*

CATHERINE: *I* don't talk to you? *She hits his arm.* What do you mean?

EDDIE: I don't see you no more. I come home you're runnin' around someplace—

CATHERINE: Well, he wants to see everything, that's all, so we go. . . . You mad at me?

EDDIE: No. *He moves from her, smiling sadly.* It's just I used to come home, you was always there. Now, I turn around, you're a big girl. I don't know how to talk to you.

CATHERINE: Why?

EDDIE: I don't know, you're runnin', you're runnin', Katie. I don't think you listening any more to me.

CATHERINE, *going to him:* Ah, Eddie, sure I am. What's the matter? You don't like him?

Slight pause.

EDDIE *turns to her: You* like him, Katie?

CATHERINE, *with a blush but holding her ground:* Yeah. I like him.

EDDIE—*his smile goes:* You like him.

CATHERINE, *looking down:* Yeah. *Now she looks at him for the consequences, smiling but tense. He looks at her like a lost boy.* What're you got against him? I don't understand. He only blesses you.

EDDIE *turns away:* He don't bless me, Katie.

CATHERINE: He does! You're like a father to him!

EDDIE *turns to her:* Katie.

CATHERINE: What, Eddie?

EDDIE: You gonna marry him?

CATHERINE: I don't know. We just been . . . goin' around, that's all. *Turns to him:* What're you got against him, Eddie? Please, tell me. What?

EDDIE: He don't respect you.

CATHERINE: Why?

EDDIE: Katie . . . if you wasn't an orphan, wouldn't he ask your father's permission before he run around with you like this?

CATHERINE: Oh, well, he didn't think you'd mind.

EDDIE: He knows I mind, but it don't bother him if I mind, don't you see that?

CATHERINE: No, Eddie, he's got all kinds of respect for me. And you too! We walk across the street he takes my arm— he almost bows to me! You got him all wrong, Eddie; I mean it, you—

EDDIE: Katie, he's only bowin' to his passport.

CATHERINE: His passport!

EDDIE: That's right. He marries you he's got the right to be an American citizen. That's what's goin' on here. *She is puzzled and surprised.* You understand what I'm tellin' you? The guy is lookin' for his break, that's all he's lookin' for.

CATHERINE, *pained:* Oh, no, Eddie, I don't think so.

EDDIE: You don't think so! Katie, you're gonna make me cry here. Is that a workin' man? What does he do with his first money? A snappy new jacket he buys, records, a pointy pair new shoes and his brother's kids are starvin' over there with tuberculosis? That's a hit-and-run guy, Baby; he's got bright lights in his head, Broadway. Them guys don't think of nobody but theirself! You marry him and the next time you see him it'll be for divorce!

CATHERINE *steps toward him:* Eddie, he never said a word about his papers or—

EDDIE: You mean he's supposed to tell you that?

CATHERINE: I don't think he's even thinking about it.

EDDIE: What's better for him to think about! He could be picked up any day here and he's back pushin' taxis up the hill!

CATHERINE: No, I don't believe it.

EDDIE: Katie, don't break my heart, listen to me.

CATHERINE: I don't want to hear it.

EDDIE: Katie, listen . . .

CATHERINE: He loves me!

EDDIE, *with deep alarm:* Don't say that, for God's sake! This is the oldest racket in the country—

CATHERINE, *desperately, as though he had made his imprint:* I don't believe it! *She rushes to the house.*

EDDIE, *following her:* They been pullin' this since the Immigration Law was put in! They grab a green kid that don't know nothin' and they—

CATHERINE, *sobbing:* I don't believe it and I wish to hell you'd stop it!

EDDIE: Katie!

They enter the apartment. The lights in the living room have risen and BEATRICE *is there. She looks past the sobbing* CATHERINE *at* EDDIE, *who in the presence of his wife, makes an awkward gesture of eroded command, indicating* CATHERINE.

EDDIE: Why don't you straighten her out?

BEATRICE, *inwardly angered at his flowing emotion, which in itself alarms her:* When are you going to leave her alone?

EDDIE: B., the guy is no good!

BEATRICE, *suddenly, with open fright and fury:* You going to leave her alone? Or you gonna drive me crazy? *He turns, striving to retain his dignity, but nevertheless in guilt walks out of the house, into the street and away. Catherine starts into a bedroom.* Listen, Catherine. *Catherine halts, turns to her sheepishly.* What are you going to do with yourself?

CATHERINE: I don't know.

BEATRICE: Don't tell me you don't know; you're not a baby any more, what are you going to do with yourself?

CATHERINE: He won't listen to me.

BEATRICE: I don't understand this. He's not your father, Catherine. I don't understand what's going on here.

CATHERINE, *as one who herself is trying to rationalize a buried impulse:* What am I going to do, just kick him in the face with it?

BEATRICE: Look, honey, you wanna get married, or don't you wanna get married? What are you worried about, Katie?

CATHERINE, *quietly, trembling:* I don't know B. It just seems wrong if he's against it so much.

BEATRICE, *never losing her aroused alarm:* Sit down, honey, I want to tell you something. Here, sit down. Was there ever any fella he liked for you? There wasn't, was there?

CATHERINE: But he says Rodolpho's just after his papers.

BEATRICE: Look, he'll say anything. What does he care what he says? If it was a prince came here for you it would be no different. You know that, don't you?

CATHERINE: Yeah, I guess.

BEATRICE: So what does that mean?

CATHERINE *slowly turns her head to Beatrice:* What?

BEATRICE: It means you gotta be your own self more. You still think you're a little girl, honey. But nobody else can make up your mind for you any more, you understand? You gotta give him to understand that he can't give you orders no more.

CATHERINE: Yeah, but how am I going to do that? He thinks I'm a baby.

BEATRICE: Because *you* think you're a baby. I told you fifty times already, you can't act the way you act. You still walk around in front of him in your slip—

CATHERINE: Well I forgot.

BEATRICE: Well you can't do it. Or like you sit on the edge of the bathtub talkin' to him when he's shavin' in his underwear.

CATHERINE: When'd I do that?

BEATRICE: I seen you in there this morning.

CATHERINE: Oh . . . well, I wanted to tell him something and I—

BEATRICE: I know, honey. But if you act like a baby and he be treatin' you like a baby. Like when he comes home sometimes you throw yourself at him like when you was twelve years old.

CATHERINE: Well I like to see him and I'm happy so I—

BEATRICE: Look, I'm not tellin' you what to do honey, but—

CATHERINE: No, you could tell me, B.! Gee, I'm all mixed up. See, I— He looks so sad now and it hurts me.

BEATRICE: Well look Katie, if it's goin' to hurt you so much you're gonna end up an old maid here.

CATHERINE: No!

BEATRICE: I'm tellin' you, I'm not makin' a joke. I tried to tell you a couple of times in the last year or so. That's why I was so happy you were going to go out and get work, you wouldn't be here so much, you'd be a little more independent. I mean it. It's wonderful for a whole family to love each other, but you're a grown woman and you're in the same house with a grown man. So you'll act different now, heh?

CATHERINE: Yeah, I will. I'll remember.

BEATRICE: Because it ain't only up to him, Katie, you understand? I told him the same thing already.

CATHERINE, *quickly*: What?

BEATRICE: That he should let you go. But, you see, if only I tell him, he thinks I'm just bawlin' him out, or maybe I'm jealous or somethin', you know?

CATHERINE, *astonished*: He said you was jealous?

BEATRICE: No, I'm just sayin' maybe that's what he thinks. *She reaches over to Catherine's hand; with a strained smile*: You think I'm jealous of you, honey?

CATHERINE: No! It's the first I thought of it.

BEATRICE, *with a quiet sad laugh:* Well you should have thought of it before . . . but I'm not. We'll be all right. Just give him to understand; you don't have to fight, you're just— You're a woman, that's all, and you got a nice boy, and now the time came when you said good-by. All right?

CATHERINE, *strangely moved at the prospect:* All right. . . . If I can.

BEATRICE: Honey . . . you gotta.

CATHERINE, *sensing now an imperious demand, turns with some fear, with a discovery, to* BEATRICE. *She is at the edge of tears, as though a familiar world had shattered.*

CATHERINE: Okay.

Lights out on them and up on ALFIERI, *seated behind his desk.*

ALFIERI: It was at this time that he first came to me. I had represented his father in an accident case some years before, and I was acquainted with the family in a casual way. I re member him now as he walked through my doorway—

Enter EDDIE *down right ramp.*

His eyes were like tunnels; my first thought was that he had committed a crime. *Eddie sits beside the desk, cap in hand, looking out.*

But soon I saw it was only a passion that had moved into his body, like a stranger. *Alfieri pauses, looks down at his desk, then to Eddie as though he were continuing a conversation with him.* I don't quite understand what I can do for you. Is there a question of law somewhere?

EDDIE: That's what I want to ask you.

ALFIERI: Because there's nothing illegal about a girl falling in love with an immigrant.

EDDIE: Yeah, but what about it if the only reason for it is to get his papers?

ALFIERI: First of all you don't know that.

EDDIE: I see it in his eyes; he's laughin' at her and he's laughin' at me.

ALFIERI: Eddie, I'm a lawyer. I can only deal in what's provable. You understand that, don't you? Can you prove that?

EDDIE: *I know what's in his mind, Mr. Alfieri!*

ALFIERI: Eddie, even if you could prove that—

EDDIE: Listen . . . will you listen to me a minute? My father always said you was a smart man. I want you to listen to me.

ALFIERI: I'm only a lawyer, Eddie.

EDDIE: Will you listen a minute? I'm talkin' about the law. Lemme just bring out what I mean. A man, which he comes into the country illegal, don't it stand to reason he's gonna take every penny and put it in the sock? Because they don't know from one day to another, right?

ALFIERI: All right.

EDDIE: He's spendin'. Records he buys now. Shoes. Jackets. Y'understand me? This guy ain't worried. This guy is *here*. So it must be that he's got it all laid out in his mind already—he's stayin'. Right?

ALFIERI: Well? What about it?

EDDIE: All right. *He glances at Alfieri, then down to the floor.* I'm talking to you confidential, ain't I?

ALFIERI: Certainly.

EDDIE: I mean it don't go no place but here. Because I don't like to say this about anybody. Even my wife I didn't exactly say this.

ALFIERI: What is it?

EDDIE *takes a breath and glances briefly over each shoulder:* The guy ain't right, Mr. Alfieri.

ALFIERI: What do you mean?

EDDIE: I mean he ain't right.

ALFIERI: I don't get you.

EDDIE *shifts to another position in the chair:* Dja ever get a look at him?

ALFIERI: Not that I know of, no.

EDDIE: He's a blond guy. Like . . . platinum. You know what I mean?

ALFIERI: No.

EDDIE: I mean if you close the paper fast—you could blow him over.

ALFIERI: Well that doesn't mean—

EDDIE: Wait a minute, I'm tellin' you sump'm. He sings, see. Which is—I mean it's all right, but sometimes he hits a note, see. I turn around. I mean—high. You know what I mean?

ALFIERI: Well, that's a tenor.

EDDIE: I know a tenor, Mr. Alfieri. This ain't no tenor. I mean if you came in the house and you didn't know who was singin', you wouldn't be lookin' for him you be lookin' for her.

ALFIERI: Yes, but that's not—

EDDIE: I'm tellin' you sump'm, wait a minute. Please, Mr. Alfieri. I'm tryin' to bring out my thoughts here. Couple of nights ago my niece brings out a dress which it's too small for her, because she shot up like a light this last year. He takes the dress, lays it on the table, he cuts it up; one-two-three, he makes a new dress. I mean he looked so sweet there, like an angel—you could kiss him he was so sweet.

ALFIERI: Now look, Eddie—

EDDIE: Mr. Alfieri, they're laughin' at him on the piers. I'm ashamed. Paper Doll they call him. Blondie now. His brother thinks it's because he's got a sense of humor, see—which he's got—but that ain't what they're laughin'. Which they're not goin' to come out with it because they know he's my relative, which they have to see me if they make a crack, y'know? But I know what they're laughin' at, and when I think of that guy layin' his hands on her I could—I mean it's eatin' me out, Mr. Alfieri, because I struggled for that girl. And now he comes in my house and—

ALFIERI: Eddie, look—I have my own children. I understand you. But the law is very specific. The law does not . . .

EDDIE, *with a fuller flow of indignation*: You mean to tell me that there's no law that a guy which he ain't right can go to work and marry a girl and—?

ALFIERI: You have no recourse in the law, Eddie.

EDDIE: Yeah, but if he ain't right, Mr. Alfieri, you mean to tell me—

ALFIERI: There is nothing you can do, Eddie, believe me.

EDDIE: Nothin'.

ALFIERI: Nothing at all. There's only one legal question here.

EDDIE: What?

ALFIERI: The manner in which they entered the country. But I don't think you want to do anything about that, do you?

EDDIE: You mean—?

ALFIERI: Well, they entered illegally.

EDDIE: Oh, Jesus, no, I wouldn't do nothin' about that, I mean—

ALFIERI: All right, then, let me talk now, eh?

EDDIE: Mr. Alfieri, I can't believe what you tell me. I mean there must be some kinda law which—

ALFIERI: Eddie, I want you to listen to me. *Pause.* You know, sometimes God mixes up the people. We all love somebody, the wife, the kids—every man's got somebody that he loves, heh? But sometimes . . . there's too much. You know? There's too much, and it goes where it mustn't. A man works hard, he brings up a child, sometimes it's a niece, sometimes even a daughter, and he never realizes it, but through the years—there is too much love for the daughter, there is too much love for the niece. Do you understand what I'm saying to you?

EDDIE, *sardonically:* What do you mean, I shouldn't look out for her good?

ALFIERI: Yes, but these things have to end, Eddie, that's all. The child has to grow up and go away, and the man has to learn to forget. Because after all, Eddie—what other way can it end? *Pause.* Let her go. That's my advice. You did your job, now it's her life; wish her luck, and let her go. *Pause.* Will you do that? Because there's no law, Eddie; make up your mind to it; the law is not interested in this.

EDDIE: You mean to tell me, even if he's a punk? If he's—

ALFIERI: There's nothing you can do.

EDDIE *stands.*

EDDIE: Well, all right, thanks. Thanks very much.

ALFIERI: What are you going to do?

EDDIE, *with a helpless but ironic gesture:* What can I do? I'm a patsy, what can a patsy do? I worked like a dog twenty years so a punk could have her, so that's what I done. I mean, in the worst times, in the worst, when there wasn't a ship comin' in the harbor, I didn't stand around lookin' for relief—I hustled. When there was empty piers in Brooklyn I went to Hoboken, Staten Island, the West Side, Jersey, all over—because I made a promise. I took out of my own mouth to give to her. I took out of my wife's mouth. I walked hungry plenty days in this city! *It begins to break through.* And now I gotta sit in my own house and look at a son-of-a-bitch punk like that—which he came out of no-where! I give him my house to sleep! I take the blankets off my bed for him, and he takes and puts his dirty filthy hands on her like a goddam thief!

ALFIERI, *rising:* But, Eddie, she's a woman now.

EDDIE: He's stealing from me!

ALFIERI: She wants to get married, Eddie. She can't marry you, can she?

EDDIE, *furiously:* What're you talkin' about, marry me! I don't know what the hell you're talkin' about!

Pause.

ALFIERI: I gave you my advice, Eddie. That's it.

EDDIE *gathers himself. A pause.*

EDDIE: Well, thanks. Thanks very much. It just—it's breakin' my heart, y'know. I—

ALFIERI: I understand. Put it out of your mind. Can you do that?

EDDIE: I'm— *He feels the threat of sobs, and with a helpless wave.* I'll see you around. *He goes out up the right ramp.*

ALFIERI *sits on desk:* There are times when you want to spread an alarm, but nothing has happened. I knew, I knew then and there—I could have finished the whole story that afternoon. It wasn't as though there was a mystery to un-

ravel. I could see every step coming, step after step, like a
dark figure walking down a hall toward a certain door. I
knew where he was heading for, I knew where he was going
to end. And I sat here many afternoons asking myself why,
being an intelligent man, I was so powerless to stop it. I even
went to a certain old lady in the neighborhood, a very wise
old woman, and I told her, and she only nodded, and said,
"Pray for him . . ." And so I—waited here.

As lights go out on ALFIERI, *they rise in the apartment
where all are finishing dinner.* BEATRICE *and* CATHERINE
are clearing the table.

CATHERINE: You know where they went?
BEATRICE: Where?
CATHERINE: They went to Africa once. On a fishing boat.
Eddie glances at her. It's true, Eddie.

BEATRICE *exits into the kitchen with dishes.*

EDDIE: I didn't say nothin'. *He goes to his rocker, picks up a
newspaper.*
CATHERINE: And I was never even in Staten Island.
EDDIE, *sitting with the paper:* You didn't miss nothin'.
Pause. Catherine takes dishes out. How long that take you,
Marco—to get to Africa?
MARCO, *rising:* Oh . . . two days. We go all over.
RODOLPHO, *rising:* Once we went to Yugoslavia.
EDDIE, *to Marco:* They pay all right on them boats?

BEATRICE *enters. She and* RODOLPHO *stack the remain-
ing dishes.*

MARCO: If they catch fish they pay all right. *Sits on a stool.*
RODOLPHO: They're family boats, though. And nobody in
our family owned one. So we only worked when one of the
families was sick.
BEATRICE: Y'know, Marco, what I don't understand—
there's an ocean full of fish and yiz are all starvin'.
EDDIE: They gotta have boats, nets, you need money.

CATHERINE *enters.*

BEATRICE: Yeah, but couldn't they like fish from the beach? You see them down Coney Island—

MARCO: Sardines.

EDDIE: Sure. *Laughing:* How you gonna catch sardines on a hook?

BEATRICE: Oh, I didn't know they're sardines. *To Catherine:* They're sardines!

CATHERINE: Yeah, they follow them all over the ocean, Africa, Yugoslavia . . . *She sits and begins to look through a movie magazine. Rodolpho joins her.*

BEATRICE, *to Eddie:* It's funny, y'know. You never think of it, that sardines are swimming in the ocean! *She exits to kitchen with dishes.*

CATHERINE: I know. It's like oranges and lemons on a tree. *To Eddie:* I mean you ever think of oranges and lemons on a tree?

EDDIE: Yeah, I know. It's funny. *To Marco:* I heard that they paint the oranges to make them look orange.

BEATRICE *enters.*

MARCO—*he has been reading a letter:* Paint?

EDDIE: Yeah, I heard that they grow like green.

MARCO: No, in Italy the oranges are orange.

RODOLPHO: Lemons are green.

EDDIE, *resenting his instruction:* I know lemons are green, for Christ's sake, you see them in the store they're green sometimes. I said oranges they paint, I didn't say nothin' about lemons.

BEATRICE, *sitting; diverting their attention:* Your wife is gettin' the money all right, Marco?

MARCO: Oh, yes. She bought medicine for my boy.

BEATRICE: That's wonderful. You feel better, heh?

MARCO: Oh, yes! But I'm lonesome.

BEATRICE: I just hope you ain't gonna do like some of them

around here. They're here twenty-five years, some men, and they didn't get enough together to go back twice.

MARCO: Oh, I know. We have many families in our town, the children never saw the father. But I will go home. Three, four years, I think.

BEATRICE: Maybe you should keep more here. Because maybe she thinks it comes so easy you'll never get ahead of yourself.

MARCO: Oh, no, she saves. I send everything. My wife is very lonesome. *He smiles shyly.*

BEATRICE: She must be nice. She pretty? I bet, heh?

MARCO, *blushing:* No, but she understand everything.

RODOLPHO: Oh, he's got a clever wife!

EDDIE: I betcha there's plenty surprises sometimes when those guys get back there, heh?

MARCO: Surprises?

EDDIE, *laughing:* I mean, you know—they count the kids and there's a couple extra than when they left?

MARCO: No—no . . . The women wait, Eddie. Most. Most. Very few surprises.

RODOLPHO: It's more strict in our town. *Eddie looks at him now.* It's not so free.

EDDIE *rises, paces up and down:* It ain't so free here either, Rodolpho, like you think. I seen greenhorns sometimes get in trouble that way—they think just because a girl don't go around with a shawl over her head that she ain't strict, y'know? Girl don't have to wear black dress to be strict. Know what I mean?

RODOLPHO: Well, I always have respect—

EDDIE: I know, but in your town you wouldn't just drag off some girl without permission, I mean. *He turns.* You know what I mean, Marco? It ain't that much different here.

MARCO, *cautiously:* Yes.

BEATRICE: Well, he didn't exactly drag her off though, Eddie.

EDDIE: I know, but I seen some of them get the wrong idea sometimes. *To Rodolpho:* I mean it might be a little more free here but it's just as strict.

RODOLPHO: I have respect for her, Eddie. I do anything wrong?

EDDIE: Look, kid, I ain't her father, I'm only her uncle—

BEATRICE: Well then, be an uncle then. *Eddie looks at her, aware of her criticizing force.* I *mean*.

MARCO: No, Beatrice, if he does wrong you must tell him. *To Eddie:* What does he do wrong?

EDDIE: Well, Marco, till he came here she was never out on the street twelve o'clock at night.

MARCO, *to Rodolpho:* You come home early now.

BEATRICE, *to Catherine:* Well, you said the movie ended late, didn't you?

CATHERINE: Yeah.

BEATRICE: Well, tell him, honey. *To Eddie:* The movie ended late.

EDDIE: Look, B., I'm just sayin'—he thinks she always stayed out like that.

MARCO: You come home early now, Rodolpho.

RODOLPHO, *embarrassed:* All right, sure. But I can't stay in the house all the time, Eddie.

EDDIE: Look, kid, I'm not only talkin' about her. The more you run around like that the more chance you're takin'. *To Beatrice:* I mean suppose he gets hit by a car or something. *To Marco:* Where's his papers, who is he? Know what I mean?

BEATRICE: Yeah, but who is he in the daytime, though? It's the same chance in the daytime.

EDDIE, *holding back a voice full of anger:* Yeah, but he don't have to go lookin' for it, Beatrice. If he's here to work, then he should work; if he's here for a good time then he could fool around! *To Marco:* But I understood, Marco, that you was both comin' to make a livin' for your family. You understand me, don't you, Marco? *He goes to his rocker.*

MARCO: I beg your pardon, Eddie.

EDDIE: I mean, that's what I understood in the first place, see.

MARCO: Yes. That's why we came.

EDDIE *sits on his rocker:* Well, that's all I'm askin'.

EDDIE *reads his paper. There is a pause, an awkward-ness. Now* CATHERINE *gets up and puts a record on the phonograph—"Paper Doll."*

CATHERINE, *flushed with revolt:* You wanna dance, Rodolpho?

EDDIE *freezes.*

RODOLPHO, *in deference to Eddie:* No, I—I'm tired.
BEATRICE: Go ahead, dance, Rodolpho.
CATHERINE: Ah, come on. They got a beautiful quartet, these guys. Come.

She has taken his hand and he stiffly rises, feeling EDDIE'*s eyes on his back, and they dance.*

EDDIE, *to Catherine:* What's that, a new record?
CATHERINE: It's the same one. We bought it the other day.
BEATRICE, *to Eddie:* They only bought three records. *She watches them dance; Eddie turns his head away. Marco just sits there, waiting. Now Beatrice turns to Eddie.* Must be nice to go all over in one of them fishin' boats. I would like that myself. See all them other countries?
EDDIE: Yeah.
BEATRICE, *to Marco:* But the women don't go along, I bet.
MARCO: No, not on the boats. Hard work.
BEATRICE: What're you got, a regular kitchen and every-thing?
MARCO: Yes, we eat very good on the boats—especially when Rodolpho comes along; everybody gets fat.
BEATRICE: Oh, he cooks?
MARCO: Sure, very good cook. Rice, pasta, fish, everything.

EDDIE *lowers his paper.*

EDDIE: He's a cook, too! *Looking at Rodolpho:* He sings, he cooks . . .

RODOLPHO *smiles thankfully.*

BEATRICE: Well it's good, he could always make a living.

EDDIE: It's wonderful. He sings, he cooks, he could make dresses . . .

CATHERINE: They get some high pay, them guys. The head chefs in all the big hotels are men. You read about them.

EDDIE: That's what I'm sayin'.

CATHERINE *and* RODOLPHO *continue dancing.*

CATHERINE: Yeah, well, I mean.

EDDIE, *to Beatrice:* He's lucky, believe me. *Slight pause. He looks away, then back to Beatrice.* That's why the water front is no place for him. *They stop dancing. Rodolpho turns off phonograph.* I mean like me—I can't cook, I can't sing, I can't make dresses, so I'm on the water front. But if I could cook, if I could sing, if I could make dresses, I wouldn't be on the water front. *He has been unconsciously twisting the newspaper into a tight roll. They are all regarding him now; he senses he is exposing the issue and he is driven on.* I would be someplace else. I would be like in a dress store. *He has bent the rolled paper and it suddenly tears in two. He suddenly gets up and pulls his pants up over his belly and goes to Marco.* What do you say, Marco, we go to the bouts next Saturday night. You never seen a fight, did you?

MARCO, *uneasily:* Only in the moving pictures.

EDDIE, *going to Rodolpho:* I'll treat yiz. What do you say, Danish? You wanna come along? I'll buy the tickets.

RODOLPHO: Sure. I like to go.

CATHERINE *goes to Eddie; nervously happy now:* I'll make some coffee, all right?

EDDIE: Go ahead, make some! Make it nice and strong. *Mystified, she smiles and exits to kitchen. He is weirdly elated, rubbing his fists into his palms. He strides to Marco.* You wait, Marco, you see some real fights here. You ever do any boxing?

MARCO: No, I never.

EDDIE, *to Rodolpho:* Betcha you have done some, heh?

RODOLPHO: No.

EDDIE: Well, come on, I'll teach you.

BEATRICE: What's he got to learn that for?

EDDIE: Ya can't tell, one a these days somebody's liable to step on his foot or sump'm. Come on, Rodolpho, I show you a couple a passes. *He stands below table.*

BEATRICE: Go ahead, Rodolpho. He's a good boxer, he could teach you.

RODOLPHO, *embarrassed:* Well, I don't know how to— *He moves down to Eddie.*

EDDIE: Just put your hands up. Like this, see? That's right. That's very good, keep your left up, because you lead with the left, see, like this. *He gently moves his left into Rodolpho's face.* See? Now what you gotta do is you gotta block me, so when I come in like that you— *Rodolpho parries his left.* Hey, that's very good! *Rodolpho laughs.* All right, now come into me. Come on.

RODOLPHO: I don't want to hit you, Eddie.

EDDIE: Don't pity me, come on. Throw it, I'll show you how to block it. *Rodolpho jabs at him, laughing. The others join.* 'At's it. Come on again. For the jaw right here. *Rodolpho jabs with more assurance.* Very good!

BEATRICE, *to Marco:* He's very good!

EDDIE *crosses directly upstage of* RODOLPHO.

EDDIE: Sure, he's great! Come on, kid, put sump'm behind it, you can't hurt me. *Rodolpho, more seriously, jabs at Eddie's jaw and grazes it.* Attaboy.

CATHERINE *comes from the kitchen, watches.*

Now I'm gonna hit you, so block me, see?

CATHERINE, *with beginning alarm:* What are they doin'?

They are lightly boxing now.

BEATRICE—*she senses only the comradeship in it now:* He's teachin' him; he's very good!

EDDIE: Sure, he's terrific! Look at him go! *Rodolpho lands a blow.* 'At's it! Now, watch out, here I come, Danish! *He feints with his left hand and lands with his right. It mildly staggers Rodolpho. Marco rises.*

CATHERINE, *rushing to Rodolpho:* Eddie!

EDDIE: Why? I didn't hurt him. Did I hurt you, kid? *He rubs the back of his hand across his mouth.*

RODOLPHO: No, no, he didn't hurt me. *To Eddie with a certain gleam and a smile:* I was only surprised.

BEATRICE, *pulling Eddie down into the rocker:* That's enough, Eddie; he did pretty good, though.

EDDIE: Yeah. *Rubbing his fists together:* He could be very good, Marco. I'll teach him again.

MARCO *nods at him dubiously.*

RODOLPHO: Dance, Catherine. Come. *He takes her hand; they go to phonograph and start it. It plays "Paper Doll."*

RODOLPHO *takes her in his arms. They dance.* EDDIE *in thought sits in his chair, and* MARCO *takes a chair, places it in front of* EDDIE, *and looks down at it.* BEATRICE *and* EDDIE *watch him.*

MARCO: Can you lift this chair?

EDDIE: What do you mean?

MARCO: From here. *He gets on one knee with one hand behind his back, and grasps the bottom of one of the chair legs but does not raise it.*

EDDIE: Sure, why not? *He comes to the chair, kneels, grasps the leg, raises the chair one inch, but it leans over to the floor.* Gee, that's hard, I never knew that. *He tries again, and again fails.* It's on an angle, that's why, heh?

MARCO: Here. *He kneels, grasps, and with strain slowly raises the chair higher and higher, getting to his feet now. Rodolpho and Catherine have stopped dancing as Marco raises the chair over his head.*

MARCO *is face to face with* EDDIE, *a strained tension gripping his eyes and jaw, his neck stiff, the chair raised like a weapon over* EDDIE'S *head—and he transforms what might appear like a glare of warning into a smile of triumph, and* EDDIE'S *grin vanishes as he absorbs his look.*

CURTAIN

ACT TWO

Light rises on ALFIERI *at his desk.*

ALFIERI: On the twenty-third of that December a case of Scotch whisky slipped from a net while being unloaded—as a case of Scotch whisky is inclined to do on the twenty-third of December on Pier Forty-one. There was no snow, but it was cold, his wife was out shopping. Marco was still at work. The boy had not been hired that day; Catherine told me later that this was the first time they had been alone together in the house.

Light is rising on CATHERINE *in the apartment.* RODOLPHO *is watching as she arranges a paper pattern on cloth spread on the table.*

CATHERINE: You hungry?

RODOLPHO: Not for anything to eat. *Pause.* I have nearly three hundred dollars. Catherine?

CATHERINE: I heard you.

RODOLPHO: You don't like to talk about it any more?

CATHERINE: Sure, I don't mind talkin' about it.

RODOLPHO: What worries you, Catherine?

CATHERINE: I been wantin' to ask you about something. Could I?

RODOLPHO: All the answers are in my eyes, Catherine. But you don't look in my eyes lately. You're full of secrets. *She looks at him. She seems withdrawn.* What is the question?

CATHERINE: Suppose I wanted to live in Italy.

RODOLPHO, *smiling at the incongruity:* You going to marry
somebody rich?

CATHERINE: No, I mean live there—you and me.

RODOLPHO, *his smile vanishing:* When?

CATHERINE: Well . . . when we get married.

RODOLPHO, *astonished:* You want to be an Italian?

CATHERINE: No, but I could live there without being Italian.
Americans live there.

RODOLPHO: Forever?

CATHERINE: Yeah.

RODOLPHO *crosses to rocker:* You're fooling.

CATHERINE: No, I mean it.

RODOLPHO: Where do you get such an idea?

CATHERINE: Well, you're always saying it's so beautiful
there, with the mountains and the ocean and all the—

RODOLPHO: You're fooling me.

CATHERINE: I mean it.

RODOLPHO *goes to her slowly:* Catherine, if I ever brought
you home with no money, no business, nothing, they would
call the priest and the doctor and they would say Rodolpho
is crazy.

CATHERINE: I know, but I think we would be happier there.

RODOLPHO: Happier! What would you eat? You can't cook
the view!

CATHERINE: Maybe you could be a singer, like in Rome or—

RODOLPHO: Rome! Rome is full of singers.

CATHERINE: Well, I could work then.

RODOLPHO: Where?

CATHERINE: God, there must be jobs somewhere!

RODOLPHO: There's nothing! Nothing, nothing, nothing.
Now tell me what you're talking about. How can I bring you
from a rich country to suffer in a poor country? What are
you talking about? *She searches for words.* I would be a crim-
inal stealing your face. In two years you would have an old,
hungry face. When my brother's babies cry they give them
water, water that boiled a bone. Don't you believe that?

CATHERINE, *quietly:* I'm afraid of Eddie here.

Slight pause.

RODOLPHO *steps closer to her:* We wouldn't live here. Once I am a citizen I could work anywhere and I would find better jobs and we would have a house, Catherine. If I were not afraid to be arrested I would start to be something wonderful here!

CATHERINE, *steeling herself:* Tell me something. I mean just tell me, Rodolpho—would you still want to do it if it turned out we had to go live in Italy? I mean just if it turned out that way.

RODOLPHO: This is your question or his question?

CATHERINE: I would like to know, Rodolpho. I mean it.

RODOLPHO: To go there with nothing.

CATHERINE: Yeah.

RODOLPHO: No. *She looks at him wide-eyed.* No.

CATHERINE: You wouldn't?

RODOLPHO: No; I will not marry you to live in Italy. I want you to be my wife, and I want to be a citizen. Tell him that, or I will. Yes. *He moves about angrily.* And tell him also, and tell yourself, please, that I am not a beggar, and you are not a horse, a gift, a favor for a poor immigrant.

CATHERINE: Well, don't get mad!

RODOLPHO: I am furious! *Goes to her.* Do you think I am so desperate? My brother is desperate, not me. You think I would carry on my back the rest of my life a woman I didn't love just to be an American? It's so wonderful? You think we have no tall buildings in Italy? Electric lights? No wide streets? No flags? No automobiles? Only work we don't have. I want to be an American so I can work, that is the only wonder here—work! How can you insult me, Catherine?

CATHERINE: I didn't mean that—

RODOLPHO: My heart dies to look at you. Why are you so afraid of him?

CATHERINE, *near tears:* I don't know!

RODOLPHO: Do you trust me, Catherine? You?

CATHERINE: It's only that I— He was good to me, Rodolpho. You don't know him; he was always the sweetest guy to me. Good. He razzes me all the time but he don't mean it. I know. I would—just feel ashamed if I made him sad. 'Cause I always dreamt that when I got married he would be happy at the wedding, and laughin'—and now he's—mad all the time and nasty— *She is weeping.* Tell him you'd live in Italy—just tell him, and maybe he would start to trust you a little, see? Because I want him to be happy; I mean—I like him, Rodolpho—and I can't stand it!

RODOLPHO: Oh, Catherine—oh, little girl.

CATHERINE: I love you, Rodolpho, I love you.

RODOLPHO: Then why are you afraid? That he'll spank you?

CATHERINE: Don't, don't laugh at me! I've been here all my life. . . . Every day I saw him when he left in the morning and when he came home at night. You think it's so easy to turn around and say to a man he's nothin' to you no more?

RODOLPHO: I know, but—

CATHERINE: You don't know; nobody knows! I'm not a baby, I know a lot more than people think I know. Beatrice says to be a woman, but—

RODOLPHO: Yes.

CATHERINE: Then why don't she be a woman? If I was a wife I would make a man happy instead of goin' at him all the time. I can tell a block away when he's blue in his mind and just wants to talk to somebody quiet and nice. . . . I can tell when he's hungry or wants a beer before he even says anything. I know when his feet hurt him, I mean I *know* him and now I'm supposed to turn around and make a stranger out of him? I don't know why I have to do that, I mean.

RODOLPHO: Catherine. If I take in my hands a little bird. And she grows and wishes to fly. But I will not let her out of my hands because I love her so much, is that right for me to do? I don't say you must hate him; but anyway you must go, mustn't you? Catherine?

CATHERINE, *softly:* Hold me.

RODOLPHO, *clasping her to him:* Oh, my little girl.

CATHERINE: Teach me. *She is weeping.* I don't know anything, teach me, Rodolpho, hold me.

RODOLPHO: There's nobody here now. Come inside. Come. *He is leading her toward the bedrooms.* And don't cry any more.

Light rises on the street. In a moment EDDIE *appears. He is unsteady, drunk. He mounts the stairs. He enters the apartment, looks around, takes out a bottle from one pocket, puts it on the table. Then another bottle from another pocket, and a third from an inside pocket. He sees the pattern and cloth, goes over to it and touches it, and turns toward upstage.*

EDDIE: Beatrice? *He goes to the open kitchen door and looks in.* Beatrice? Beatrice?

CATHERINE *enters from bedroom; under his gaze she adjusts her dress.*

CATHERINE: You got home early.

EDDIE: Knocked off for Christmas early. *Indicating the pattern:* Rodolpho makin' you a dress?

CATHERINE: No. I'm makin' a blouse.

RODOLPHO *appears in the bedroom doorway.* EDDIE *sees him and his arm jerks slightly in shock.* RODOLPHO *nods to him testingly.*

RODOLPHO: Beatrice went to buy presents for her mother.

Pause.

EDDIE: Pack it up. Go ahead. Get your stuff and get outa here. *Catherine instantly turns and walks toward the bedroom, and Eddie grabs her arm.* Where you goin'?

CATHERINE, *trembling with fright:* I think I have to get out of here, Eddie.

EDDIE: No, you ain't goin' nowhere, he's the one.

CATHERINE: I think I can't stay here no more. *She frees her arm, steps back toward the bedroom.* I'm sorry, Eddie. *She sees the tears in his eyes.* Well, don't cry. I'll be around the neighborhood; I'll see you. I just can't stay here no more. You know I can't. *Her sobs of pity and love for him break her composure.* Don't you know I can't? You know that, don't you? *She goes to him.* Wish me luck. *She clasps her hands prayerfully.* Oh, Eddie, don't be like that!

EDDIE: You ain't goin' nowheres.

CATHERINE: Eddie, I'm not gonna be a baby any more! You—

He reaches out suddenly, draws her to him, and as she strives to free herself he kisses her on the mouth.

RODOLPHO: Don't! *He pulls on Eddie's arm.* Stop that! Have respect for her!

EDDIE, *spun round by Rodolpho:* You want something?

RODOLPHO: Yes! She'll be my wife. That is what I want. My wife!

EDDIE: But what're you gonna be?

RODOLPHO: I show you what I be!

CATHERINE: Wait outside; don't argue with him!

EDDIE: Come on, show me! What're you gonna be? Show me!

RODOLPHO, *with tears of rage:* Don't say that to me!

RODOLPHO *flies at him in attack.* EDDIE *pins his arms, laughing, and suddenly kisses him.*

CATHERINE: Eddie! Let go, ya hear me! I'll kill you! Leggo of him!

She tears at EDDIE's *face and* EDDIE *releases* RODOLPHO. EDDIE *stands there with tears rolling down his face as he laughs mockingly at* RODOLPHO. *She is staring at him in horror.* RODOLPHO *is rigid. They are like animals that have torn at one another and broken up without a decision, each waiting for the other's mood.*

EDDIE, *to Catherine:* You see? *To Rodolpho:* I give you till tomorrow, kid. Get outa here. Alone. You hear me? Alone.

CATHERINE: I'm going with him, Eddie. *She starts toward Rodolpho.*

EDDIE, *indicating Rodolpho with his head:* Not with that.

She halts, frightened. He sits, still panting for breath, and they watch him helplessly as he leans toward them over the table. Don't make me do nuttin', Catherine. Watch your step, submarine. By rights they oughta throw you back in the water. But I got pity for you. *He moves unsteadily toward the door, always facing Rodolpho.* Just get outa here and don't lay another hand on her unless you wanna go out feet first. *He goes out of the apartment.*

The lights go down, as they rise on ALFIERI.

ALFIERI: On December twenty-seventh I saw him next. I normally go home well before six, but that day I sat around looking out my window at the bay, and when I saw him walking through my doorway, I knew why I had waited. And if I seem to tell this like a dream, it was that way. Several moments arrived in the course of the two talks we had when it occurred to me how—almost transfixed I had come to feel. I had lost my strength somewhere. *Eddie enters, removing his cap, sits in the chair, looks thoughtfully out.* I looked in his eyes more than I listened—in fact, I can hardly remember the conversation. But I will never forget how dark the room became when he looked at me; his eyes were like tunnels. I kept wanting to call the police, but nothing had happened. Nothing at all had really happened. *He breaks off and looks down at the desk. Then he turns to Eddie.* So in other words, he won't leave?

EDDIE: My wife is talkin' about renting a room upstairs for them. An old lady on the top floor is got an empty room.

ALFIERI: What does Marco say?

EDDIE: He just sits there. Marco don't say much.

ALFIERI: I guess they didn't tell him, heh? What happened?

EDDIE: I don't know; Marco don't say much.

ALFIERI: What does your wife say?

EDDIE, *unwilling to pursue this:* Nobody's talkin' much in the house. So what about that?

ALFIERI: But you didn't prove anything about him. It sounds like he just wasn't strong enough to break your grip.

EDDIE: I'm tellin' you I know—he ain't right. Somebody that don't want it can break it. Even a mouse, if you catch a teeny mouse and you hold it in your hand, that mouse can give you the right kind of fight. He didn't give me the right kind of fight, I know it, Mr. Alfieri, the guy ain't right.

ALFIERI: What did you do that for, Eddie?

EDDIE: To show her what he is! So she would see, once and for all! Her mother'll turn over in the grave! *He gathers himself almost peremptorily.* So what do I gotta do now? Tell me what to do.

ALFIERI: She actually said she's marrying him?

EDDIE: She told me, yeah. So what do I do?

Slight pause.

ALFIERI: This is my last word, Eddie, take it or not, that's your business. Morally and legally you have no rights, you cannot stop it; she is a free agent.

EDDIE, *angering:* Didn't you hear what I told you?

ALFIERI, *with a tougher tone:* I heard what you told me, and I'm telling you what the answer is. I'm not only telling you now, I'm warning you—the law is nature. The law is only a word for what has a right to happen. When the law is wrong it's because it's unnatural, but in this case it is natural and a river will drown you if you buck it now. Let her go. And bless her. *A phone booth begins to glow on the opposite side of the stage; a faint, lonely blue. Eddie stands up, jaws clenched.* Somebody had to come for her, Eddie, sooner or later. *Eddie starts turning to go and Alfieri rises with new anxiety.* You won't have a friend in the world, Eddie! Even those who understand will turn against you, even the ones who feel the same will despise you! *Eddie moves off.* Put it out of your mind! Eddie! *He follows into the darkness, calling desperately.*

EDDIE *is gone. The phone is glowing in light now. Light is out on* ALFIERI. EDDIE *has at the same time appeared beside the phone.*

EDDIE: Give me the number of the Immigration Bureau. Thanks. *He dials.* I want to report something. Illegal immigrants. Two of them. That's right. Four-forty-one Saxon Street, Brooklyn, yeah. Ground floor. Heh? *With greater difficulty:* I'm just around the neighborhood, that's all. Heh?

Evidently he is being questioned further, and he slowly hangs up. He leaves the phone just as LOUIS *and* MIKE *come down the street.*

LOUIS: Go bowlin', Eddie?
EDDIE: No, I'm due home.
LOUIS: Well, take it easy.
EDDIE: I'll see yiz.

They leave him, exiting right, and he watches them go. He glances about, then goes up into the house. The lights go on in the apartment. BEATRICE *is taking down Christmas decorations and packing them in a box.*

EDDIE: Where is everybody? *Beatrice does not answer.* I says where is everybody?
BEATRICE, *looking up at him, wearied with it, and concealing a fear of him:* I decided to move them upstairs with Mrs. Dondero.
EDDIE: Oh, they're all moved up there already?
BEATRICE: Yeah.
EDDIE: Where's Catherine? She up there?
BEATRICE: Only to bring pillow cases.
EDDIE: She ain't movin' in with them.
BEATRICE: Look, I'm sick and tired of it. I'm sick and tired of it!
EDDIE: All right, all right, take it easy.
BEATRICE: I don't wanna hear no more about it, you understand? Nothin'!
EDDIE: What're you blowin' off about? Who brought them in here?
BEATRICE: All right, I'm sorry; I wish I'd a drop dead before I told them to come. In the ground I wish I was.

EDDIE: Don't drop dead, just keep in mind who brought them in here, that's all. *He moves about restlessly.* I mean I got a couple of rights here. *He moves, wanting to beat down her evident disapproval of him.* This is my house here not their house.

BEATRICE: What do you want from me? They're moved out; what do you want now?

EDDIE: I want my respect!

BEATRICE: So I moved them out, what more do you want? You got your house now, you got your respect.

EDDIE—*he moves about biting his lip:* I don't like the way you talk to me, Beatrice.

BEATRICE: I'm just tellin' you I done what you want!

EDDIE: I don't like it! The way you talk to me and the way you look at me. This is my house. And she is my niece and I'm responsible for her.

BEATRICE: So that's why you done that to him?

EDDIE: I done what to him?

BEATRICE: What you done to him in front of her; you know what I'm talkin' about. She goes around shakin' all the time, she can't go to sleep! That's what you call responsible for her?

EDDIE, *quietly:* The guy ain't right, Beatrice. *She is silent.* Did you hear what I said?

BEATRICE: Look, I'm finished with it. That's all. *She resumes her work.*

EDDIE, *helping her to pack the tinsel:* I'm gonna have it out with you one of these days, Beatrice.

BEATRICE: Nothin' to have out with me, it's all settled. Now we gonna be like it never happened, that's all.

EDDIE: I want my respect, Beatrice, and you know what I'm talkin' about.

BEATRICE: What?

Pause.

EDDIE—*finally his resolution hardens:* What I feel like doin' in the bed and what I don't feel like doin'. I don't want no—

BEATRICE: When'd I say anything about that?

EDDIE: You said, you said, I ain't deaf. I don't want no more conversations about that, Beatrice. I do what I feel like doin' or what I don't feel like doin'.

BEATRICE: Okay.

Pause.

EDDIE: You used to be different, Beatrice. You had a whole different way.

BEATRICE: *I'm* no different.

EDDIE: You didn't used to jump me all the time about everything. The last year or two I come in the house I don't know what's gonna hit me. It's a shootin' gallery in here and I'm the pigeon.

BEATRICE: Okay, okay.

EDDIE: Don't tell me okay, okay, I'm tellin' you the truth. A wife is supposed to believe the husband. If I tell you that guy ain't right don't tell me he is right.

BEATRICE: But how do you know?

EDDIE: Because I know. I don't go around makin' accusations. He give me the heeby-jeebies the first minute I seen him. And I don't like you sayin' I don't want her marryin' anybody. I broke my back payin' her stenography lessons so she could go out and meet a better class of people. Would I do that if I didn't want her to get married? Sometimes you talk like I was a crazy man or sump'm.

BEATRICE: But she likes him.

EDDIE: Beatrice, she's a baby, how is she gonna know what she likes?

BEATRICE: Well, you kept her a baby, you wouldn't let her go out. I told you a hundred times.

Pause.

EDDIE: All right. Let her go out, then.

BEATRICE: She don't wanna go out now. It's too late, Eddie.

Pause.

EDDIE: Suppose I told her to go out. Suppose I—

BEATRICE: They're going to get married next week, Eddie.

EDDIE—*his head jerks around to her:* She said that?

BEATRICE: Eddie, if you want my advice, go to her and tell her good luck. I think maybe now that you had it out you learned better.

EDDIE: What's the hurry next week?

BEATRICE: Well, she's been worried about him bein' picked up; this way he could start to be a citizen. She loves him, Eddie. *He gets up, moves about uneasily, restlessly.* Why don't you give her a good word? Because I still think she would like you to be a friend, y'know? *He is standing, looking at the floor.* I mean like if you told her you'd go to the wedding.

EDDIE: She asked you that?

BEATRICE: I know she would like it. I'd like to make a party here for her. I mean there oughta be some kinda send-off. Heh? I mean she'll have trouble enough in her life, let's start it off happy. What do you say? Cause in her heart she still loves you, Eddie. I know it. *He presses his fingers against his eyes.* What're you, cryin'? *She goes to him, holds his face.* Go . . . whyn't you go tell her you're sorry? *Catherine is seen on the upper landing of the stairway, and they hear her descending.* There . . . she's comin' down. Come on, shake hands with her.

EDDIE, *moving with suppressed suddenness:* No, I can't, I can't talk to her.

BEATRICE: Eddie, give her a break; a wedding should be happy!

EDDIE: I'm goin', I'm goin' for a walk.

He goes upstage for his jacket. CATHERINE *enters and starts for the bedroom door.*

BEATRICE: Katie? . . . Eddie, don't go, wait a minute. *She embraces Eddie's arm with warmth.* Ask him, Katie. Come on, honey.

EDDIE: It's all right, I'm— *He starts to go and she holds him.*

BEATRICE: No, she wants to ask you. Come on, Katie, ask

him. We'll have a party! What're we gonna do, hate each other? Come on!

CATHERINE: I'm gonna get married, Eddie. So if you wanna come, the wedding be on Saturday.

Pause.

EDDIE: Okay. I only wanted the best for you, Katie. I hope you know that.

CATHERINE: Okay. *She starts out again.*

EDDIE: Catherine? *She turns to him.* I was just tellin' Beatrice . . . if you wanna go out, like . . . I mean I realize maybe I kept you home too much. Because he's the first guy you ever knew, y'know? I mean now that you got a job, you might meet some fellas, and you get a different idea, y'know? I mean you could always come back to him, you're still only kids, the both of yiz. What's the hurry? Maybe you'll get around a little bit, you grow up a little more, maybe you'll see different in a couple of months. I mean you be surprised, it don't have to be him.

CATHERINE: No, we made it up already.

EDDIE, *with increasing anxiety:* Katie, wait a minute.

CATHERINE: No, I made up my mind.

EDDIE: But you never knew no other fella, Katie! How could you make up your mind?

CATHERINE: Cause I did. I don't want nobody else.

EDDIE: But, Katie, suppose he gets picked up.

CATHERINE: That's why we gonna do it right away. Soon as we finish the wedding he's goin' right over and start to be a citizen. I made up my mind, Eddie. I'm sorry. *To Beatrice:* Could I take two more pillow cases for the other guys?

BEATRICE: Sure, go ahead. Only don't let her forget where they came from.

CATHERINE *goes into a bedroom.*

EDDIE: She's got other boarders up there?

BEATRICE: Yeah, there's two guys that just came over.

EDDIE: What do you mean, came over?

BEATRICE: From Italy. Lipari the butcher—his nephew. They come from Bari, they just got here yesterday. I didn't even know till Marco and Rodolpho moved up there before. *Catherine enters, going toward exit with two pillow cases.* It'll be nice, they could all talk together.

EDDIE: Catherine! *She halts near the exit door. He takes in Beatrice too.* What're you, got no brains? You put them up there with two other submarines?

CATHERINE: Why?

EDDIE, *in a driving fright and anger:* Why! How do you know they're not trackin' these guys? They'll come up for them and find Marco and Rodolpho! Get them out of the house!

BEATRICE: But they been here so long already—

EDDIE: How do you know what enemies Lipari's got? Which they'd love to stab him in the back?

CATHERINE: Well what'll I do with them?

EDDIE: The neighborhood is full of rooms. Can't you stand to live a couple of blocks away from him? Get them out of the house!

CATHERINE: Well maybe tomorrow night I'll—

EDDIE: Not tomorrow, do it now. Catherine, you never mix yourself with somebody else's family! These guys get picked up, Lipari's liable to blame you or me and we got his whole family on our head. They got a temper, that family.

Two men in overcoats appear outside, start into the house.

CATHERINE: How'm I gonna find a place tonight?

EDDIE: Will you stop arguin' with me and get them out! You think I'm always tryin' to fool you or sump'm? What's the matter with you, don't you believe I could think of your good? Did I ever ask sump'm for myself? You think I got no feelin's? I never told you nothin' in my life that wasn't for your good. Nothin'! And look at the way you talk to me! Like I was an enemy! Like I— *A knock on the door. His head swerves. They all stand motionless. Another knock. Eddie, in a whisper, pointing upstage.* Go up the fire escape, get them out over the back fence.

CATHERINE *stands motionless, uncomprehending.*

FIRST OFFICER, *in the hall:* Immigration! Open up in there!

EDDIE: Go, go. Hurry up! *She stands a moment staring at him in a realized horror.* Well, what're you lookin' at!

FIRST OFFICER: Open up!

EDDIE, *calling toward door:* Who's that there?

FIRST OFFICER: Immigration, open up.

EDDIE *turns, looks at* BEATRICE. *She sits. Then he looks at* CATHERINE. *With a sob of fury* CATHERINE *streaks into a bedroom.*
  Knock is repeated.

EDDIE: All right, take it easy, take it easy. *He goes and opens the door. The Officer steps inside.* What's all this?

FIRST OFFICER: Where are they?

SECOND OFFICER *sweeps past and, glancing about, goes into the kitchen.*

EDDIE: Where's who?

FIRST OFFICER: Come on, come on, where are they? *He hurries into the bedrooms.*

EDDIE: Who? We got nobody here. *He looks at Beatrice, who turns her head away. Pugnaciously, furious, he steps toward Beatrice.* What's the matter with *you?*

FIRST OFFICER *enters from the bedroom, calls to the kitchen.*

FIRST OFFICER: Dominick?

Enter SECOND OFFICER *from kitchen.*

SECOND OFFICER: Maybe it's a different apartment.

FIRST OFFICER: There's only two more floors up there. I'll take the front, you go up the fire escape. I'll let you in. Watch your step up there.

SECOND OFFICER: Okay, right, Charley. *First Officer goes*

out apartment door and runs up the stairs. This is
Four-forty-one, isn't it?

EDDIE: That's right.

SECOND OFFICER *goes out into the kitchen.*

  EDDIE *turns to* BEATRICE. *She looks at him now and
sees his terror.*

BEATRICE, *weakened with fear:* Oh, Jesus, Eddie.

EDDIE: What's the matter with *you?*

BEATRICE, *pressing her palms against her face:* Oh, my God,
my God.

EDDIE: What're you, accusin' me?

BEATRICE—*her final thrust is to turn toward him instead of
running from him:* My God, what did you do?

Many steps on the outer stair draw his attention. We see the
FIRST OFFICER *descending, with* MARCO, *behind him*
RODOLPHO, *and* CATHERINE *and the two strange immigrants, followed by* SECOND OFFICER. BEATRICE
hurries to door.

CATHERINE, *backing down stairs, fighting with First Officer; as they appear on the stairs:* What do yiz want from
them? They work, that's all. They're boarders upstairs, they
work on the piers.

BEATRICE, *to First Officer:* Ah, Mister, what do you want
from them, who do they hurt?

CATHERINE, *pointing to Rodolpho:* They ain't no submarines, he was born in Philadelphia.

FIRST OFFICER: Step aside, lady.

CATHERINE: What do you mean? You can't just come in a
house and—

FIRST OFFICER: All right, take it easy. *To Rodolpho:* What
street were you born in Philadelphia?

CATHERINE: What do you mean, what street? Could you tell
me what street you were born?

FIRST OFFICER: Sure. Four blocks away, One-eleven Union
Street. Let's go fellas.

CATHERINE, *fending him off Rodolpho:* No, you can't! Now, get outa here!

FIRST OFFICER: Look, girlie, if they're all right they'll be out tomorrow. If they're illegal they go back where they came from. If you want, get yourself a lawyer, although I'm tellin' you now you're wasting your money. Let's get them in the car, Dom. *To the men:* Andiamo, andiamo, let's go.

The men start, but MARCO *hangs back.*

BEATRICE, *from doorway:* Who're they hurtin', for God's sake, what do you want from them? They're starvin' over there, what do you want! Marco!

MARCO *suddenly breaks from the group and dashes into the room and faces* EDDIE; BEATRICE *and* FIRST OFFICER *rush in as* MARCO *spits into* EDDIE's *face.*

CATHERINE *runs into hallway and throws herself into* RODOLPHO's *arms.* EDDIE, *with an enraged cry, lunges for* MARCO.

EDDIE: Oh, you mother's—!

FIRST OFFICER *quickly intercedes and pushes* EDDIE *from* MARCO, *who stands there accusingly.*

FIRST OFFICER, *between them, pushing Eddie from Marco:* Cut it out!

EDDIE, *over the First Officer's shoulder, to Marco:* I'll kill you for that, you son of a bitch!

FIRST OFFICER: Hey! *Shakes him.* Stay in here now, don't come out, don't bother him. You hear me? Don't come out, fella.

For an instant there is silence. Then FIRST OFFICER *turns and takes* MARCO's *arm and then gives a last, informative look at* EDDIE. *As he and* MARCO *are going out into the hall,* EDDIE *erupts.*

EDDIE: I don't forget that, Marco! You hear what I'm sayin'?

Out in the hall, FIRST OFFICER *and* MARCO *go down the stairs. Now, in the street,* LOUIS, MIKE, *and several neighbors including the butcher,* LIPARI—*a stout, intense, middle-aged man—are gathering around the stoop.*

LIPARI, *the butcher, walks over to the two strange men and kisses them. His wife, keening, goes and kisses their hands.* EDDIE *is emerging from the house shouting after* MARCO. BEATRICE *is trying to restrain him.*

EDDIE: That's the thanks I get? Which I took the blankets off my bed for yiz? You gonna apologize to me, Marco! *Marco!*

FIRST OFFICER, *in the doorway with Marco:* All right, lady, let them go. Get in the car, fellas, it's over there.

RODOLPHO *is almost carrying the sobbing* CATHERINE *off up the street, left.*

CATHERINE: He was born in Philadelphia! What do you want from him?

FIRST OFFICER: Step aside, lady, come on now . . .

The SECOND OFFICER *has moved off with the two strange men.* MARCO, *taking advantage of the* FIRST OFFICER's *being occupied with* CATHERINE, *suddenly frees himself and points back at* EDDIE.

MARCO: That one! I accuse that one!

EDDIE *brushes* BEATRICE *aside and rushes out to the stoop.*

FIRST OFFICER, *grabbing him and moving him quickly off up the left street:* Come on!

MARCO, *as he is taken off, pointing back at Eddie:* That one! He killed my children! That one stole the food from my children!

MARCO *is gone. The crowd has turned to* EDDIE.

EDDIE, *to Lipari and wife:* He's crazy! I give them the blankets off my bed. Six months I kept them like my own brothers!

LIPARI, *the butcher, turns and starts up left with his arm around his wife.*

EDDIE: Lipari! *He follows Lipari up left.* For Christ's sake, I kept them, I give them the blankets off my bed!

LIPARI *and wife exit.* EDDIE *turns and starts crossing down right to* LOUIS *and* MIKE.

EDDIE: Louis! *Louis!*

LOUIS *barely turns, then walks off and exits down right with* MIKE. *Only* BEATRICE *is left on the stoop.* CATHERINE *now returns, blank-eyed, from offstage and the car.* EDDIE *calls after* LOUIS *and* MIKE.

EDDIE: He's gonna take that back. He's gonna take that back or I'll kill him! You hear me? I'll kill him! I'll kill him! *He exits up street calling.*

There is a pause of darkness before the lights rise, on the reception room of a prison. MARCO *is seated;* ALFIERI, CATHERINE, *and* RODOLPHO *standing.*

ALFIERI: I'm waiting, Marco, what do you say?

RODOLPHO: Marco never hurt anybody.

ALFIERI: I can bail you out until your hearing comes up. But I'm not going to do it, you understand me? Unless I have your promise. You're an honorable man, I will believe your promise. Now what do you say?

MARCO: In my country he would be dead now. He would not live this long.

ALFIERI: All right, Rodolpho—you come with me now.

RODOLPHO: No! Please, Mister. Marco—promise the man. Please, I want you to watch the wedding. How can I be married and you're in here? Please, you're not going to do anything; you know you're not.

MARCO *is silent.*

CATHERINE, *kneeling left of Marco:* Marco, don't you understand? He can't bail you out if you're gonna do some-

thing bad. To hell with Eddie. Nobody is gonna talk to him
again if he lives to a hundred. Everybody knows you spit in
his face, that's enough, isn't it? Give me the satisfaction—I
want you at the wedding. You got a wife and kids, Marco.
You could be workin' till the hearing comes up, instead of
layin' around here.

MARCO, *to Alfieri:* I have no chance?

ALFIERI *crosses to behind Marco:* No, Marco. You're going
back. The hearing is a formality, that's all.

MARCO: But him? There is a chance, eh?

ALFIERI: When she marries him he can start to become an
American. They permit that, if the wife is born here.

MARCO, *looking at Rodolpho:* Well—we did something. *He
lays a palm on Rodolpho's arm and Rodolpho covers it.*

RODOLPHO: Marco, tell the man.

MARCO, *pulling his hand away:* What will I tell him? He
knows such a promise is dishonorable.

ALFIERI: To promise not to kill is not dishonorable.

MARCO, *looking at Alfieri:* No?

ALFIERI: No.

MARCO, *gesturing with his head—this is a new idea:* Then
what is done with such a man?

ALFIERI: Nothing. If he obeys the law, he lives. That's all.

MARCO *rises, turns to Alfieri:* The law? All the law is not in
a book.

ALFIERI: Yes. In a book. There is no other law.

MARCO, *his anger rising:* He degraded my brother. My blood.
He robbed my children, he mocks my work. I work to come
here, mister!

ALFIERI: I know, Marco—

MARCO: There is no law for that? Where is the law for that?

ALFIERI: There is none.

MARCO, *shaking his head, sitting:* I don't understand this
country.

ALFIERI: Well? What is your answer? You have five or six
weeks you could work. Or else you sit here. What do you
say to me?

MARCO *lowers his eyes. It almost seems he is ashamed.* All right.

ALFIERI: You won't touch him. This is your promise.

Slight pause.

MARCO: Maybe he wants to apologize to me.

MARCO *is staring away.* ALFIERI *takes one of his hands.*

ALFIERI: This is not God, Marco. You hear? Only God makes justice.

MARCO: All right.

ALFIERI, *nodding, not with assurance:* Good! Catherine, Rodolpho, Marco, let us go.

CATHERINE *kisses* RODOLPHO *and* MARCO, *then kisses* ALFIERI's *hand.*

CATHERINE: I'll get Beatrice and meet you at the church. *She leaves quickly.*

MARCO *rises.* RODOLPHO *suddenly embraces him.* MARCO *pats him on the back and* RODOLPHO *exits after* CATHERINE. MARCO *faces* ALFIERI.

ALFIERI: Only God, Marco.

MARCO *turns and walks out.* ALFIERI *with a certain processional tread leaves the stage. The lights dim out.*
    The lights rise in the apartment. EDDIE *is alone in the rocker, rocking back and forth in little surges. Pause. Now* BEATRICE *emerges from a bedroom. She is in her best clothes, wearing a hat.*

BEATRICE, *with fear, going to Eddie:* I'll be back in an hour, Eddie. All right?

EDDIE, *quietly, almost inaudibly, as though drained:* What, have I been talkin' to myself?

BEATRICE: Eddie, for God's sake, it's her wedding.

EDDIE: Didn't you hear what I told you? You walk out that door to that wedding you ain't comin' back here, Beatrice.

BEATRICE: Why! What do you want?

EDDIE: I want my respect. Didn't you ever hear of that? From my wife?

CATHERINE *enters from bedroom.*

CATHERINE: It's after three; we're supposed to be there already, Beatrice. The priest won't wait.

BEATRICE: Eddie. It's her wedding. There'll be nobody there from her family. For my sister let me go. I'm goin' for my sister.

EDDIE, *as though hurt:* Look, I been arguin' with you all day already, Beatrice, and I said what I'm gonna say. He's gonna come here and apologize to me or nobody from this house is goin' into that church today. Now if that's more to you than I am, then go. But don't come back. You be on my side or on their side, that's all.

CATHERINE, *suddenly:* Who the hell do you think you are?

BEATRICE: Sssh!

CATHERINE: You got no more right to tell nobody nothin'! Nobody! The rest of your life, nobody!

BEATRICE: Shut up, Katie! *She turns Catherine around.*

CATHERINE: You're gonna come with me!

BEATRICE: I can't Katie, I can't . . .

CATHERINE: How can you listen to him? This rat!

BEATRICE, *shaking Catherine:* Don't you call him that!

CATHERINE, *clearing from Beatrice:* What're you scared of? He's a rat! He belongs in the sewer!

BEATRICE: Stop it!

CATHERINE, *weeping:* He bites people when they sleep! He comes when nobody's lookin' and poisons decent people. In the garbage he belongs!

EDDIE *seems about to pick up the table and fling it at her.*

BEATRICE: No, Eddie! Eddie! *To Catherine:* Then we all belong in the garbage. You, and me too. Don't say that. Whatever happened we all done it, and don't you ever forget it, Catherine. *She goes to Catherine.* Now go, go to your wedding, Katie, I'll stay home. Go. God bless you, God bless your children.

Enter RODOLPHO.

RODOLPHO: Eddie?

EDDIE: Who said you could come in here? Get outa here!

RODOLPHO: Marco is coming, Eddie. *Pause. Beatrice raises her hands in terror.* He's praying in the church. You understand? *Pause. Rodolpho advances into the room.* Catherine, I think it is better we go. Come with me.

CATHERINE: Eddie, go away, please.

BEATRICE, *quietly:* Eddie, let's go someplace. Come. You and me. *He has not moved.* I don't want you to be here when he comes. I'll get your coat.

EDDIE: Where? Where am I goin'? This is my house.

BEATRICE, *crying out:* What's the use of it! He's crazy now, you know the way they get, what good is it! You got nothin' against Marco, you always liked Marco!

EDDIE: I got nothin' against Marco? Which he called me a rat in front of the whole neighborhood? Which he said I killed his children! Where you been?

RODOLPHO, *quite suddenly, stepping up to Eddie:* It is my fault, Eddie. Everything. I wish to apologize. It was wrong that I do not ask your permission. I kiss your hand. *He reaches for Eddie's hand, but Eddie snaps it away from him.*

BEATRICE: Eddie, he's apologizing!

RODOLPHO: I have made all our troubles. But you have insult me too. Maybe God understand why you did that to me. Maybe you did not mean to insult me at all—

BEATRICE: Listen to him! Eddie, listen what he's tellin' you!

RODOLPHO: I think, maybe when Marco comes, if we can tell him we are comrades now, and we have no more argument between us. Then maybe Marco will not—

EDDIE: Now, listen—

CATHERINE: Eddie, give him a chance!

BEATRICE: What do you want! Eddie, what do you want!

EDDIE: I want my name! He didn't take my name; he's only a

punk. Marco's got my name—*to Rodolpho:* and you can run tell him, kid, that he's gonna give it back to me in front of this neighborhood, or we have it out. *Hoisting up his pants:* Come on, where is he? Take me to him.

BEATRICE: Eddie, listen—

EDDIE: I heard enough! Come on, let's go!

BEATRICE: Only blood is good? He kissed your hand!

EDDIE: What he does don't mean nothin' to nobody! *To Rodolpho:* Come on!

BEATRICE, *barring his way to the stairs:* What's gonna mean somethin'? Eddie, listen to me. Who could give you your name? Listen to me, I love you, I'm talkin' to you, I love you; if Marco'll kiss your hand outside, if he goes on his knees, what is he got to give you? That's not what you want.

EDDIE: Don't bother me!

BEATRICE: You want somethin' else, Eddie, and you can never have her!

CATHERINE, *in horror:* B.!

EDDIE, *shocked, horrified, his fist clenching:* Beatrice!

MARCO *appears outside, walking toward the door from a distant point.*

BEATRICE, *crying out, weeping:* The truth is not as bad as blood, Eddie! I'm tellin' you the truth—tell her good-by forever!

EDDIE, *crying out in agony:* That's what you think of me— that I would have such a thought? *His fists clench his head as though it will burst.*

MARCO, *calling near the door outside:* Eddie Carbone!

EDDIE *swerves about; all stand transfixed for an instant. People appear outside.*

EDDIE, *as though flinging his challenge:* Yeah, Marco! Eddie Carbone. Eddie Carbone. Eddie Carbone. *He goes up the stairs and emerges from the apartment. Rodolpho streaks up and out past him and runs to Marco.*

RODOLPHO: No, Marco, please! Eddie, please, he has children! You will kill a family!

BEATRICE: Go in the house! Eddie, go in the house!

EDDIE—*he gradually comes to address the people:* Maybe he come to apologize to me. Heh, Marco? For what you said about me in front of the neighborhood? *He is incensing himself and little bits of laughter even escape him as his eyes are murderous and he cracks his knuckles in his hands with a strange sort of relaxation.* He knows that ain't right. To do like that? To a man? Which I put my roof over their head and my food in their mouth? Like in the Bible? Strangers I never seen in my whole life? To come out of the water and grab a girl for a passport? To go and take from your own family like from the stable—and never a word to me? And now accusations in the bargain! *Directly to Marco:* Wipin' the neighborhood with my name like a dirty rag! I want my name, Marco. *He is moving now, carefully, toward Marco.* Now gimme my name and we go together to the wedding.

BEATRICE *and* CATHERINE, *keening:* Eddie! Eddie, don't! Eddie!

EDDIE: No, Marco knows what's right from wrong. Tell the people, Marco, tell them what a liar you are! *He has his arms spread and Marco is spreading his.* Come on, liar, you know what you done! *He lunges for Marco as a great hushed shout goes up from the people.*

MARCO *strikes* EDDIE *beside the neck.*

MARCO: Animal! You go on your knees to me!

EDDIE *goes down with the blow and* MARCO *starts to raise a foot to stomp him when* EDDIE *springs a knife into his hand and* MARCO *steps back.* LOUIS *rushes in toward* EDDIE.

LOUIS: Eddie, for Christ's sake!

EDDIE *raises the knife and* LOUIS *halts and steps back.*

EDDIE: You lied about me, Marco. Now say it. Come on now, say it!

MARCO: Anima-a-a-l!

EDDIE *lunges with the knife.* MARCO *grabs his arm, turning the blade inward and pressing it home as the women and* LOUIS *and* MIKE *rush in and separate them, and* EDDIE, *the knife still in his hand, falls to his knees before* MARCO. *The two women support him for a moment, calling his name again and again.*

CATHERINE: Eddie I never meant to do nothing bad to you.
EDDIE: Then why— Oh, B.!
BEATRICE: Yes, yes!
EDDIE: My B.!

He dies in her arms, and BEATRICE *covers him with her body.* ALFIERI, *who is in the crowd, turns out to the audience. The lights have gone down, leaving him in a glow, while behind him the dull prayers of the people and the keening of the women continue.*

ALFIERI: Most of the time now we settle for half and I like it better. But the truth is holy, and even as I know how wrong he was, and his death useless, I tremble, for I confess that something perversely pure calls to me from his memory— not purely good, but himself purely, for he allowed himself to be wholly known and for that I think I will love him more than all my sensible clients. And yet, it is better to settle for half, it must be! And so I mourn him—I admit it—with a certain . . . alarm.

CURTAIN

PENGUIN MODERN CLASSICS

THE CRUCIBLE
ARTHUR MILLER

'One of a handful of great plays that will both survive the twentieth century and bear witness to it' John Peter, *Sunday Times*

Arthur Miller's classic parable of mass hysteria draws a chilling parallel between the Salem witch-hunt of 1692 – 'one of the strangest and most awful chapters in human history' – and the McCarthyism which gripped America in the 1950s. The story of how the small community of Salem is stirred to madness by superstition, paranoia and malice, culminating in a violent climax, is a savage attack on the evils of mindless persecution and the terrifying power of false accusations.

Penguin Modern Classics

AFTER THE FALL
ARTHUR MILLER

'Endlessly fascinating, emotionally harrowing, and consumingly committed to telling the truth as Miller sees it' *Time*

Quentin is a successful lawyer in New York, but inside his head he is struggling with his own sense of guilt and the shadows of his past relationships. One of these is an ill-fated marriage to the charming and beautiful Maggie, who went from operating a switchboard to become a self-destructive star – a singer everyone wanted a piece of.

With tremendous psychological acuity and depth, and a brilliant, dreamlike structure, *After the Fall* is a literary masterpiece – the story of a man striving to comprehend his feelings for his friends, family and the women he has loved.

Contemporary ... Provocative ... Outrageous ...
Prophetic ... Groundbreaking ... Funny ... Disturbing ...
Different ... Moving ... Revolutionary ... Inspiring ...
Subversive ... Life-changing ...

What makes a modern classic?

At Penguin Classics our mission has always been to make the best
books ever written available to everyone. And that also means
constantly redefining and refreshing exactly what makes a 'classic'.
That's where Modern Classics come in. Since 1961 they have been an
organic, ever-growing and ever-evolving list of books from the last
hundred (or so) years that we believe will continue to be read over and
over again.

They could be books that have inspired political dissent, such as
Animal Farm. Some, like *Lolita* or *A Clockwork Orange*, may have
caused shock and outrage. Many have led to great films, from *In Cold
Blood* to *One Flew Over the Cuckoo's Nest*. They have broken down
barriers – whether social, sexual, or, in the case of *Ulysses*, the
boundaries of language itself. And they might – like *Goldfinger* or
Scoop – just be pure classic escapism. Whatever the reason, Penguin
Modern Classics continue to inspire, entertain and enlighten millions
of readers everywhere.

'No publisher has had more influence on reading habits than Penguin'
Independent

'Penguins provided a crash course in world literature'
Guardian

The best books ever written

P E N G U I N 🐧 C L A S S I C S

SINCE 1946

Find out more at www.penguinclassics.com